Ability Development
From Age Zero

Saino Kaihatsu Wa Zero-Sai Kara

© Shinichi Suzuki, 1969

Original Japanese Edition

Published by

Shufunotomo Co., Ltd., 1969

English Translation Published by

Ability Development Associates, Inc.

© 1981

ISBN: 0-918194-12-1
Cover Design: Paul Bradford
Lithographed in the United States of America by
Lawhead Press, Inc., Athens, Ohio

Ability Development From Age Zero

by Shinichi Suzuki

English Translation by
Mary Louise Nagata

 A Senzay Edition

by Ability Development Associates, Inc.
subsidiary of Accura Music
Athens, Ohio, U.S.A.

Foreword

This is a book for all who are responsible for the nurturing of young children. In its translation from the original Japanese, the oriental flavor has been retained, but its perspective will stimulate new ways of viewing our educational system and our relationship with our children.

Although the literate parent has more than enough reading material to guide him in child rearing, much of it focuses on existing problems and meeting something called the child's "needs." In contrast, Suzuki's book places emphasis on the responsibility of the adult to improve everything under his control and create an environment worthy of the noble spirit with which every child is born. The dozens of stories and personal reflections not only lead to suggestions for parental consideration, but make fascinating reading as well.

This book was written in the late 1960's, primarily for parents, and without benefit of scientific clinical studies. Nevertheless, its message is clear and valid. Ultimate ability, or potential, simply cannot be determined at birth. Suzuki asks us to assume that the newborn baby has limitless capabilities and it is in the hands of the parents to provide the environment which will lead to full development of that potential.

Shinichi Suzuki was born in Nagoya, Japan, in October, 1898. He is known throughout the world as the founder of the Talent Education Movement, the most visible aspect of which has been the musical training of very young children to a high degree of proficiency on a string instrument or piano.

Suzuki has been described as a humanitarian as well as an educator and musician. While a young man, he observed that children absorbed their spoken language according to their environment. This led him to adapt his teaching of music to the same approach, now called the Mother Tongue Approach. With this system, he has established that talent or ability in any field is not inherited, but is a product of environment. Every child can learn to perform music just as he has learned to speak, provided the same teaching approach is used.

In his concern for all humanity, Suzuki has dedicated his life to improving educational methods. Convinced that enthusiasm to learn can be sustained indefinitely if the teaching method is correct, he appealed for early education "from age zero" long before modern psychologists popularized the idea.

His interest in education subsequently resulted in the formation of the Early Development Association in Japan, where there is continuous research into the learning abilities of what we know as the pre-school child.

Since 1964, he has made repeated visits to the United States and Canada to work with teachers and students and to talk to parents about the education of their children.

Lorraine Fink
May, 1981

Clarification

The words *talent* and *ability* are used in a broad sense and refer to one's capacity to think, act, or feel in any given situation. Their use is not restricted to the artistic field, but is also applied to personality traits. Thus Suzuki, and this book, will refer to the fact that one has developed the *ability* to be argumentative, the *ability* to be personable, the *talent* for being considerate, or the *talent* for being happy.

Table of Contents

Preface

In the Beginning

When someone says "Talent is not inborn," most people think, "That cannot be true."

Some thirty years ago, I also believed that talent was inborn. "I was not born with enough talent to become great," I thought. A long time ago, I noticed that this common way of thinking was a mistake. Since then I have spent some thirty years proving a method about which it can truly be said, "Look, advanced ability can be nurtured in any child. With this method wonderful ability can be developed, but with some other methods, some children will become miserable human beings with little ability." The result is that today I can say, "Talent is not inborn."

I understand that obviously any healthy child could far surpass the old standards since, "Every child grows in the same way as he is brought up." For this reason, the early education a child receives between birth and kindergarten or elementary school is very important because it controls the child's future.

In the agricultural world, success depends upon the quality of cultivation which a seed receives from the time it is planted. Human ability will not exist if it is ignored when in the seedling stage.

However, many people will still feel that the problem is more complicated than, "Every child grows in the same way he is reared."

"Is every child the same?"

I am asked, "Is there no superior ability or inferior ability?" I did not say, "All children are the same." There is no mistake in the genetical rule that there are no two people alike on earth. I am only saying that, "Inborn greatness or mediocrity is not known." Even when standing right in front of a newborn baby, it cannot be determined whether the baby has superior or inferior ability.

Until recently, public opinion has been based upon results. Educated abilities have been mistaken for inborn abilities. The results of several years of education do not show the *inborn* ability of a baby.

Every healthy child in Japan has the ability to speak excellent Japanese by the age of six or seven. It is the very way they were raised. This shows that every child has plenty of developmental possibilities.

How can talent, or ability, be nurtured? How can children be brought up to be human beings with excellent talents and beautiful hearts? Please, for the sake of your children, let them live through my research and experience.

My heartfelt belief is that, "The fate of a child is in the hands of his parents."

Shinichi Suzuki
October, 1971

Chapter 1

Talent Is Not Inborn

Everyone Has a Sprout of Talent

Through science we can fly to the moon, yet man has hardly begun to evaluate mankind. This imbalance is a reversal of that which is important and that which is trivial.

We should know our abilities, draw them out, and develop them. When this important duty is neglected, how can we say we live in a civilized world? Man's talent is not inborn.

Some people state:

"It is natural to grow up because nature is inborn."

"Nothing can be done about a lack of inborn ability."

In this fashion, *inborn* is used in good and bad ways. However, please stop and think a bit. Does not *inborn* seem to be used too quickly, too easily, too often?

When we say children have inborn ability, often those children already have been nurtured to the age of five or six. When looking at a newborn baby, absolutely nobody can say, "This child will be a talented musician," or, "This child will be a talented literary person."

Saying what is the inborn ability of a five or six year old child cannot be the same as what we mean when speaking of the inborn ability of an infant. Instead, it should be called the results of education, because it is the grown form of a five or six year old that is being observed.

Re-evaluate the school of thought which mistakenly calls the results of education as inborn ability. Start from scratch and think about the talent of man. What kind of person is the newborn child and what kind of talent is hidden within him? This is what I hope to see re-evaluated.

All Japanese Children Speak Japanese!

When the root to this idea occurred to me some twenty-five or twenty-six years ago, I was overwhelmed by the fact that all children in Japan speak Japanese easily.

"Of course they do . . . It's nothing to be surprised about," is what people say to me with skeptical eyes. However, for me it was an enlightening thought. Five and six year old children speak Japanese easily. They speak the difficult dialects of their respective areas such as the Osaka, Aomori, and Kagoshima dialects without any problem. They have the talent to catch the delicate nuances of the Osaka dialect and the ability to master the nasal pronunciation of Aomori and Akita dialects. I was astounded; this ability is no small accomplishment. The children show such a high level of educational possibilities.

Already, at five and six years old, children have developed and internalized language, and I was deeply moved by this discovery which led to my understanding of the education involved in learning the mother tongue.

"Children in Japan speak Japanese so well. How wonderful it is!" I could not help telling every friend I could find. However, whomever I met looked at me suspiciously and said, "What are you talking about? Of course they do."

Nevertheless, my astonishment was clear. All of my thoughts about the Mother Tongue Method began at that time, and my heart overflowed with happiness. Even though people thought I was crazy, I continued to talk about the surprise. I talked about it so much that people began to laugh at me.

I need to explain my surprise at seeing children speak Japanese freely. Such a high level of development seemed to show a successful education method which works unconsciously. I also profited from the strong belief that any child has seeds of ability which can be nurtured as far as the capacity of the brain will allow.

It is so commonplace for children to speak their own language that people tend to ignore it and not really look at the facts. Possibly I was so stimulated when taking note of such a happening because at that time I had been thinking seriously about a new music education method. In a way it was a flash of inspiration.

Mother Tongue Education Is the Best Method

To speak Japanese well, children must develop their language ability to a very high level. One cannot simply say that Japanese children speak Japanese because they are Japanese. If an American spoke Japanese as well as Japanese children do, it would be called a brilliant language ability. Yet a baby starts from scratch at birth and by five or six years of age has internalized the language. Here is a wonderful method of education. The best method in the world is hidden within the mother tongue education, I thought. This event should fit into all education methods. I began to search. Then, at last I decided, "If a child speaks his language fluently, he has developmental possibilities. Other abilities should therefore develop according to the way he is raised."

I ask all mothers, "Does your child speak well?" If the answer is "Yes," then I say, "If so, then that is the evidence that your child can develop excellent abilities with a good education. Have confidence."

Man grows in the same way he is reared. Man can develop to a high level according to the way he is raised. Every child can be educated, but children are not born with education. Knowing this fact will become the basis for insights regarding the nature of mankind.

Ability Breeds Ability

Let us think deeper about the way a child learns Japanese. Let us consider, for instance, the number of times a baby hears the Japanse word *Uma, Uma,** before he begins to say it, and what form the acceleration curve for word acquisition takes until he begins to say other words such as *Mama* or *Papa*. From this we can see that there is an almost uncountable number of times that the baby will hear *Uma Uma* before he is able to say it. Then that ability must grow a great deal more before he can say *Mama* or *Papa* and have a three word vocabulary. While practicing these three words, his ability must again grow a great deal so as to add a fourth word, and yet again to add a fifth. Here we can see that ability is breeding ability.

Since this explanation may be confusing, I will note the standard education procedure here:

"Do you understand?"

"Yes."

"Then let's go on."

Suppose that a baby learned Japanese in the same way?

"If you can say *Uma Uma* today . . . yes, then next . . ." The next day he learns *Mama* and the next *Papa*.

If babies were taught Japanese in this way, no one would say happily that his child had a good memory. If on a particular day one cannot remember how to say the word which was learned the day before, one will only

---

*One of the earliest terms acquired by infants for food.

learn to speak the word of the day. With this method, there are big problems.

However, education of Japanese does not involve only learning Japanese in bits and pieces. It also involves developing the *ability to learn* [emphasis added] a language at the same time. Until now, the majority of education methods have concentrated merely upon teaching in bits and pieces instead of nurturing talent.

"If I use this wonderful language education method, surely I will get good results. I shall use the method of ability breeding ability." I began to get moving.

Everyone has a sprout of talent. Developing that sprout into a wonderful ability depends upon how it is cultivated.

Even Tone Deaf Children Can Be Developed

Toshiya Eto was my first experiment. Beginning with him, the number of my pupils grew quickly.

I also taught a six-year-old tone deaf child who was successfully able to develop talent. The tone deaf child was not born that way. When he was a baby, his mother or grandmother sang out-of-tune lullabies to him, and as he heard them he became tone deaf. To cure the child's tone deafness, I used the following method:

It is very difficult to correct tone deafness which has become internalized. Therefore, instead of correcting the old tone deaf gamut,* I made a new gamut for which I repeated the training over and over again. When the new gamut had been experienced more times than the old gamut, the old gamut gradually wore thin and was erased. That child nurtured his talent so well as to have a recital in Canada. I would like parents to use their perceptive abilities to think about the seed of talent which children have that can be developed to a surprisingly high level.

*a series of recognized musical notes

I would like every parent to experience the surprise that I had when I suddenly realized how easily every child speaks Japanese. I would also have them believe that human ability is nurtured.

If I may say so, parents who say, "My child has no musical talent," or "My child is so weak in literature," are ignorant. If it is known that talent is not inborn but nurtured, then such things cannot be said. The parent who complains about his child is actually announcing to society that he has bad methods for nurturing.

Saying "My child has no talent" is actually the same as saying "I did not educate my child to develop the sprout of his talent."

The Life Force for Environmental Adaptation

One more time I shall give an example that talent is not inborn. Suppose Mozart had been given to me to care for soon after his birth. And further suppose that instead of having the influence of his wonderful musician father, Mozart heard me play an old, bent, out-of-tune record for his lullaby when he cried. Then, if Mozart listened to an out-of-tune record every day and was raised in this environment, Mozart would have internalized the out-of-tuneness and become a tone deaf person.

Even a Mozart had the possibility of becoming tone deaf depending upon the way he was raised. It is not a matter of having inborn musical talent, but rather that of internalizing the talents from the surrounding living environment.

Listen to Famous Works From Birth

How would the opposite method work? The truth is, that is what I have spent some thirty years of experimentation to discover.

Instead of playing an out-of-tune record or singing an out-of-tune lullaby for a baby, play a beautiful record regardless of the difficulty. One five minute piece. Decide upon one and play it whenever the baby cries. Play whatever the mother likes. It might be an orchestra, or any piece by Beethoven, or Mozart. Experimentation has shown that the baby will have the piece completely memorized in five months. This may be surprising, but it is true.

Try this experiment to check: Tape a piece that the baby has never heard with the piece to which he has been listening. Then play the tape for the baby. When the baby hears the new piece, he will have a look of incredulity on his face, but when the familiar piece plays he will smile and begin to move to the beat. It is a five-month-old baby, but there is nothing about which to be surprised.

Until now, education has been based upon intelligence. New knowledge is assumed to be added on top of a basic knowledge. The evidence I have cannot be explained by thinking this way.

I think that the energy of man's survival instinct acquires ability as it adapts to the environment. This idea has been well received in America as "Suzuki's Theory."

Every day a baby listens to his mother's and father's words in his environment. Mother is the one who is with the baby most often and who embraces the baby every day. Therefore the baby's life force will absorb her voice along with every other aspect of the mother. Just like a tape recorder catches the sound of a hundred piece orchestra on a tape, a baby will use his survival instinct to absorb everything in his environment while learning to be a human being. Each time something happens nearby, the development of the baby will be affected. He becomes tone deaf if out-of-tune notes are nearby. His voice will be low if his mother's voice is low. Often on the telephone the daughter cannot be distinguished from her mother.

This happens because the daughter used her life force to catch her mother's voice while still a baby.

Talent can be defined as something acquired through the physiological conditioning of a baby. Suppose I take a small child born in Tokyo to Alaska. He cannot adapt to the cold with only one month in Alaska. He will only have experienced that Alaska is a cold place. However, if he has felt the cold wind upon his body every day of his life, physiologically he will have skin which can endure cold, and his bodily functions will be tempered to the cold while the ability to endure cold is internalized by his life force striving to survive.

The strong influence of music is the same as the situation in Alaska. Music is vibrating air. Therefore, it is similar to wind. A baby acquires the ability to feel music. Acquiring the ability to feel beautiful music or discordant music is decided by the music in the environment of the baby.

The Child's Face Shows His Parents' History

If parents fight or argue with each other or raise their voices near the baby, such emotional output will be absorbed by the baby and he will adapt to that influence. A child of five months has the ability to memorize a violin concerto and can also store up the basic preparation for fighting with his spouse when he marries.

When a baby is born to a happy couple soon after their marriage, the entire household is filled with happiness because he is the first child. The child is brought up seeing the rich look of a smiling, motherly face. That baby will have an attractive face. Making a face cannot be taught, but comes about naturally through adaptation to the environment. The personality of the child is also made in this manner.

However, suppose a baby is born to a middle aged couple. Sometimes the father goes out and does not come home at night, the couple has a strained relationship, and the household is sad. This is also the first baby, but no laughing is heard from him and he is brought up with a tearful, gloomy mother. In this case the baby will have a gloomy, flat expression on his face, and his personality will be similar. The environment determines the person. This is very scary.

In lectures, I often say the following to parents: "Today when you return home, place all of your children in a row. Then if the two of you look at each of their faces in order of birth, you will see the history of your life together as a married couple written upon the faces of your children." It is with such surprising power that a baby replies in physical form to the environment at his birth.

From the day of birth the most powerful influence in the environment is the mother. Of course, the father has influence also, but through being held and breast-fed during babyhood the mother-child connection is so strong as to be unseverable, and is held together by the living force. This living force is indescribably strong. Therefore the mother-child relationship of a breast-fed child is different from that of a bottle-fed child. The personality, the actions, and all other expressions from the parent are caught by some invisible power of the baby, who gradually patterns himself as a human being.

Even the Difficult Pronunciation of R

I went to Germany when I was 23. Because I went suddenly, without studying any German, I had a very difficult time with German pronunciation. For some reason I could not pronounce *R*. At my lodgings there were three children who tried to teach me how to say *R*. They would tell me to put my tongue down, not to touch the roof of my mouth, and with an open mouth say *RRR* as they did. Always instead of *RRR*, I ended up saying *AAA*.

German children are not especially taught. During babyhood a parent says words with *RRR* in them like *doktor* many times so that the *RRR* sound enters the ears of a child many times. When we Japanese say *doktor*, we are unable to pronounce the *RRR* at the end.

Children can catch any difficult pronunciation. Concentration upon this very powerful life force is what education should be. I suggest that the combined energies of parents and teachers be concentrated on this powerful force for a wonderful education. Knowing that children have such a wonderful life force, it is inexcusable not to develop it. (I want to shout this fact many times when I think that this life force is the root of education.)

Most of the parents in the world know the physical and psychological problems of raising children well. However, the majority of people do not even think about how best to raise a child to have a fine personality and excellent abilities. This thoughtlessness is the same as throwing a child away just as he is born.

Children Are Seedlings

If adults are considered full-grown plants, then children are seedlings. Unless the seedlings are well cared for, beautiful flowers cannot be expected.

Setting a child aside until elementary school age and then saying that now education begins is like taking a withered or withering sprout and suddenly giving it large amounts of fertilizer, putting it in the sunlight and flooding it with water. It is too late for the withered sprout.

Man has been given the good fortune of a powerful life force and limitless possibilities. It is an inexcusable fault of ours to throw these away unnoticed. Every loving parent has the wish to make his child admirable and happy. However, most parents unconsciously spoil their children or make them unhappy. This happens because they are unable to recognize the powerful life force in their children.

For example, when a child receives poor grades in school, his parents and even his teachers do not doubt that the child is stupid, or not very smart. Yet this same child speaks his own language fluently. How can this fact be explained? The child is not stupid, but he was not reared well.

Suppose we have a normal baby. Further, suppose that we bind the right hand of this baby until he is four years old. If we then try to have the baby use his right hand it will not be developed well. The hand will be useless. The left hand will be well developed and the child will be left-handed. Leaving the talents of a child alone until he is four years old is like binding his right hand.

It is sad that parents all over the world do this very thing without a second thought. The fate of a child is in the hands of his parents. Unfortunately there are many children who are set aside in this manner.

It All Depends on How Children Are Raised

How about the habit of practicing the violin?

"Practice!" mother says enthusiastically every day. Regardless of how much interest mother has, nothing will happen if the child does not want to practice. "Practice!" even if repeated, is only an everyday unpleasant experience to the child. The more, "It's practice time," is said, the more the child wants to run away and play.

Please remember that ability cannot be developed without a certain amount of training. Taking a baby to Alaska for one month is not enough, but after two or three years the ability to adapt to the cold will become internalized. In order to carry out the repetition, the circumstances surrounding the repetition must be happy and without fuss.

In Talent Education, we have the mother play the record many, many times of the piece to be practiced later. There was one mother who taped the piece many times and left the tape going by itself. If the tape is playing in one part of the house, she can do other things or relax, and the child will come to think nothing of listening to the piece. During repeated listening the child will internalize the piece. Then, when the child is taken to his first violin lesson, he can hear other children playing that piece.

"I Want to Play, Too"

If a child is three years old, his mother is taught good violin posture and how to play on the small violin. The child amuses himself until the mother learns to play a short piece. After a month or two the child is probably thinking something like this: "Other children are playing the violin. I want to play, too."

At this point the child is motivated to play the violin and begins to take the violin that mother has been playing. If this happens, the child is caught. He now has the incentive to begin serious practice and the preparatory situation has been completed.

"Do you want to play the violin?" asks Mother.

"Yes," is always the answer.

"Will you work hard?"

"Yes."

"Shall we ask teacher to teach you?"

"Yes."

In this way, practice begins with a spontaneous plea from the child. Commands like, "Do your homework! Study!" when the child has no incentive, is the worst education method.

Practice that Creates Dislike

In many cases I wonder if this poor kind of practice is going on. "Do your practicing." There are those who think that this constant nagging is education. This method can be called the "How Not to Develop Ability" method.

Children will do what they dislike if they are scolded. However, if they do not have the desire to do it, it will not develop into an ability. When a child has the desire, the ability will become internalized. His life force will reach out and the ability becomes internalized.

The same can be said about plant cultivation. True cultivators know that a seed needs plenty of fertilizer, water and sunshine. If you hold a seed in your hand and yell, "Sprout! Sprout! Sprout!" you are being merciless to the seed. The seed will not sprout unless the conditions are right.

Adults typically behave in this way. I often say to mothers, "How obedient children are. Adults do such cruel things in comparison. In spite of complaints, children practice the violin every day and gradually become able to play. What would happen if they were adults? If you were scolded in the same fashion, you would turn around and scold back saying, 'I will never touch the violin again!' Children practice in spite of being scolded. Why don't you make happiness part of their incentive?"

If the attitude of the mother changes, then the attitude of the child will also change. Then he can reach out and grow more and more.

An Orange Crate Concert

I further request the following from parents:

"The child has become able to play a piece very well. After supper on Saturday of this week, make Father the audience, and Mother and child should get up on stage and play the piece for Father. Even an orange crate will

do for the stage." When this is planned, the child practices very hard to play for Father.

The Saturday night concert begins. The child bows
and plays a piece. "Very good! Well done!" Father
praises the child even if the performance was poor. Then
he says, "Would you play for me again next week?" The
child will then happily practice hard for another week.

This is one way to put incentive and joy into practice. In this way the household also becomes joyful. Only
three minutes are necessary. So much was accomplished.
It is not difficult. Beforehand, Mother says to Father,
"Please say that you wish to hear him again next week
and please applaud." In this way, even a small performance will allow the child to enjoy his practice.

The following week, the piece is more polished when
the child opens his concert. In this way, as the weeks go
by, and if other pieces the child has played are added, he
will become able to play all of his pieces well.

Once a month or once a week, the children can have
a group lesson. Children enjoy playing together very
much. It is fun to play together in ensemble. Scolding is
absent and they all play together without hesitation. Since
more advanced students will also be playing, their advanced style will be absorbed by the newer children, not
just the sound but also the stance. Through their ability
to adapt to the environment, they can pick up something
better than themselves with sensitivity and joy.

Chapter 2

Talent is Developed in This Way

Repeatedly Aim for Better Things

The ability to adapt to the environment grows. When there is training and repetition, there are good things and bad things. Both beautiful things and ugly things become internalized. This is the basic rule. Bad things develop in a bad environment and ugly things develop in an ugly environment entirely unconsciously.

Parents should aim to develop good things in their children and think of what is necessary for their happiness. Then these necessities must repeatedly be given to their children.

Mere repetition is not enough. Only bad and ugly things develop from thoughtless repetition.

A Talent Education Classroom Experiment

The following experiment was carried out by Shigeki Tanaka at the Hongo Elementary School Talent Education Classroom in Matsumoto.

"I would like these forty children without exception to develop abilities through education. They all speak Japanese fluently so they have the capacity to learn," I said to Mr. Tanaka. I requested the development of abilities in both mathematics and language.

Here is a glimpse at the mathematical training. First, tables were made for addition, subtraction, multiplication and division. During the physical education period the children said the addition table instead of counting off, *i.e.*, 1 + 1 = 2, 2 + 2 = 4, 3 + 3 = 6. Then ten problems were given to all of the children. Everyone had a score of 100 percent. The next day the same problems were given in a different order. The children who had finished in one minute finished in thirty seconds, while those who had finished in three minutes finished in two minutes. The speed showed how their ability had developed.

One day I went to visit the classroom. In the second grade class a work sheet that consisted of sixty problems was completed by most children in one minute. A child would go and get another sixty problems upon completion.

There was only one slow child present among them. When this girl entered school, she was unable to count beyond three. After daily training she managed a score of 100 percent. However, she always took three minutes to complete the problems. The other children were three times faster than she was. In other words, the children were doing 180 problems in three minutes. When I watched the slow child closely, I found that she had less concentration than the other children. She would complete twenty problems and then rest by looking out the window. Then, recalling that she had more to do, she would complete another twenty problems and rest again. Her attention span lasted for twenty problems only. Her ability was growing but she lacked concentration.

Restlessness Is Due to a Lack of Ability

Perhaps ability is proportional to the length of concentration, I thought. The ability to concentrate for long periods of time can be nurtured. Nurturing is the basis for developing ability.

Mothers often say, "My child just cannot concentrate on one thing. When I think he is doing one thing, he goes somewhere else and begins another. He is so restless that I do not know what to do." This is thought to be characteristic of children. However, it is only because children do not yet have the ability to concentrate.

"Lady, you must make the ability for your child. Have him do something on which he can concentrate. Otherwise, he will continue to be restless," I answer.

The children at Hongo Elementary School entered fourth grade. "Please come and see the length of concentration the children have." At this invitation from Mr. Tanaka, I again visited the school. Mr. Tanaka said to the children, "Today, do as many problems as you like." A mountain of problems was piled on each desk.

"Ready . . . Go!" and forty children set aside one page after another as they answered the problems. There was no sound. The concentration was tremendous and no one thought about anything except doing the problems.

I watched silently. Gradually time passed until two and one half hours had gone by.

"I understand now," I said. "This is plenty. To work for two and one half hours without tiring is doing very well. They can do it because the problems are interesting. Even if all that you did was to give them the confidence that in the future they can accomplish anything they try, it is enough."

I felt grateful to Mr. Tanaka for giving the children such confidence in themselves. Indeed, the children could continue for two and one half hours because they could do all of the problems.

The children were interested in giving answers. They enjoyed themselves immensely and were proud because they could solve all of the problems. It is fun to test oneself as to how far one can go. If the children could not do several problems in a row, they would stop.

The Joy of Developing Talent

Please remember that those children were not picked because they were special. They were a common mixture of children. That class was chosen by lots from four classes. Furthermore, it would be wrong to ignore the girl who was unable to count beyond three. Mr. Tanaka managed to succeed without exception in giving ability to each child.

I asked more about the slow child and found that she was from a coal mining home in the mountains. She had not had the benefits of a usual environment and had not been taught anything about numbers before entering school.

When she was in second grade, her face looked blank. Her face was expressionless because her mind was not working. By the time she entered the fourth grade she was on the same level as the other children. Her concentration had become longer and her facial expressions were normal.

This child was thought to be the least likely to succeed, yet later she passed the entrance exam to one of the most difficult schools. Even the ability of a child who could not count to three could be developed. It developed while absorbing as much happiness as possible. This child confirms that ability breeds and develops ability.

Here is where parents and teachers must do some thinking. Children learn abilities best when they are having fun. Use this as a weapon and repeatedly give them as much as they can do. Praise them when they do as much as they can. Then their incentive will become much stronger. If the parent or teacher then asks in the midst of praise, "Can you do any better?" the face of the child will light up as he answers, "I think that I can do much better."

Try it. Surely you will succeed.

Develop Talent Carefully

In many cases, parents and teachers present a child with tasks which the child both dislikes and cannot do. It would be better if the child was presented fun tasks which he can do and developed his ability that way. Tasks which are done happily are internalized and in this manner talent is grown carefully. This is the secret for parents and teachers regarding education.

The educational objective changes with the abilities of each child. Suppose that I have collected the answer sheets to a language exercise and that there are a number of students who finished without a mistake. Of those children, some finished early, some finished late, some breezed through the exercise easily, and some finished each question with much deliberation. If I check their papers carefully and properly, I will check their handwriting also. If a child is able to write neatly formed letters, he should be praised for that ability and encouraged to become better so that his motivation will increase. "Your mother writes so nicely. Can you do as well as she can?"

Develop ability from what the child can already do and that ability will promote the happiness of doing things better and better. An unlimited amount of ability can develop when parent and child are having fun together. This is simple but often overlooked.

Dice and the Learning Disabled Child

Here is another case which shows that happiness develops ability.

There was one child in my family with a learning disability. His mother scolded him very much when he was six. She said that he would not remember what she taught him. For some reason he could not remember the numbers from one to ten.

"Why don't you understand? This is four and this is seven!" she scolded harshly as I watched.

"It will not do any good to scold him," I warned. After some observation, I realized that four and seven were numbers that the child was scolded about and therefore he could not look at them clearly.

"Hey, come and play with your uncle," I called. Then I made dice out of paper and on the faces I wrote only fours and sevens.

"Let's play dice," I said, and we started to throw.

A four was thrown.

"Four! I said it first. I win," I said. Again a four was thrown.

"Four! I won again." At this point the little boy was determined to try harder. Again a four was thrown and together we said, "Four!"

"Hey, you said it too!" I praised. His eyes began to sparkle. The game continued with both fours and sevens being thrown. Sometimes I said the answer slowly. Sometimes I pretended that I did not know the answer and let the boy win. Sometimes I said the wrong one and the boy made no mistake. In this way four and seven became his favorite numbers in a mere ten minutes.

I had the mother write the numbers from one to ten and have the child read them. He said four and seven the quickest and in the loudest voice. These numbers had become the most well known and fun numbers.

The problem is how to combine interest and training. If a child is always scolded about four and seven, his ability will not grow. Even if a parent overflowing with love for a child uses a bad method, the ability of the child will not develop.

Feel As the Child Does

Adults may want to teach numbers or mathematics, but a child wants to be petted and have fun playing. If training can be combined with the fun, a child has the power to do things which surprise adults. Numbers must be known and mathematics must be learned. However, it is a mistake to expect a child to naturally do things from the adult world. Skillfulness in rearing a child comes from knowing and feeling as he does in his heart.

Here are the conditions for developing great ability.

1. Begin as early as possible.
2. Create the best possible environment.
3. Use the finest teaching method.
4. Provide a great deal of training.
5. Use the finest teachers.

When all of these conditions are working together, the flower of really wonderful ability will bloom.

The child is often blamed when his ability does not develop, but we must realize that it is only when the child is taught in the wrong way that the ability does not develop. Adults, not the children, are to blame. When we realize this point I think that children will have a much better chance for development. Then instead of moaning, "My child is so mischievous!" a mother will say, "My child has developed a great ability for mischief." The ability of a child can be found if looked for. We should remember that such ability can be directed into better areas, and then we can have hope even for mischievous children. The scolding a child receives for doing a prank may cause him to do an even worse prank. In this way a child might be moved in the wrong direction.

No Voice, No Finger Movement

Both good and bad effects can result from training. Here is one example:

When I first started experimenting with Talent Education violin in Matsumoto, I had a four-year-old student. This child practiced with his mother at home and she was teaching him to put down his fingers for the first variation of *Twinkle, Twinkle Little Star*.

Usually the rhythm *Taka taka ta ta* is played on the open *A* and then the open *E* strings respectively. Then the mother says *one* and the child puts the first finger on the string. This mother had the child say "Taka taka ta ta, Taka taka ta ta, one," and putting his first finger on the string, would have him play *Taka taka ta ta* twice to practice. The child was saying the words everyday during practice.

When the child came for a lesson, he played very well saying *one* or *three* for the respective fingers. He had practiced well.

"You practiced well. Now play once without speaking," I said. The result was that the fingers would not move unless he said *one* or *three*. The practice of speaking before putting down those fingers resulted in the fingers not moving without the voice. At the time, I was amazed that the child developed exactly in the way he was taught. "Now practice putting down your fingers without speaking," I said, and it took a full two weeks to repair that training.

A child develops exactly in the way he is taught. This is very scary. If I tried to develop the habit of putting down my fingers only after I spoke, I could not do it. Yet a four-year-old child did it by adapting to his environment.

In this case the bad effect was only minor, but if a very poor teaching method were to be used, the bad effects would become internalized and trying to repair them would be very discouraging.

Give My Regards to Kreisler

We cannot forget about sensitivity when thinking about ability. In violin, for example, both technique and sensitivity are necessary.

No matter how well I play for a student, it will be different to hear a world famous violinist like Kreisler playing the same piece. Therefore, I have children listen to the performances of Kreisler many times while I teach them the technique of violin playing and tone production. In this way, children will surpass the sensitivity of my own performance, internalize the sensitivity of Kreisler, and maybe even surpass him. I teach them how to study, but Kreisler teaches them musical sensitivity.

A recording of the piece the student is practicing—a recording of Kreisler, for instance—should be played for the child at home. After the lesson I ask, "Who is your teacher?" and the student answers, "Kreisler." Then I laugh and say, "Give my regards to Kreisler." What I mean is that Kreisler is the teacher. The student should have a lesson with him everyday. I want the student to know that I am only helping him in his lessons with Kreisler. The children will be happy and proud because they are the students of the best in the world. Further, by listening to good music continuously, they will internalize it.

I even followed the same practice in front of observers. After the lesson I asked the child, "Who is your teacher?" The observers had incredulous looks. The child answered, "Grumiaux." "Give my regards to Grumiaux," I said. The observers looked at me with peculiar looks on their faces.

"You have Kreisler or Grumiaux stay at your house and play many times. It is rude not to offer even one cup of tea to them. Therefore, I pay them respect by sending my greetings," I said jokingly to explain. In this way the children do not think that they are listening to just a record. They are listening to the performance of a great artist. Their love and respect for music becomes deeper.

The children who were raised in this way thirty years ago are mostly concertmasters of orchestras in America, Germany, and Canada today. This makes me happy.

Those students studied from Kreisler. They are not my students. I am only their helper. They have been internalizing the sensitivity of the best in the world since they were small children.

Adults Must Self-Reflect

Parents should always reflect to determine whether they are good Kreislers for their children. Reflection is necessary in the routine, the behavior, and the conversation of adults. Parents must constantly ask themselves whether they are good examples for their children. In other words, a parent should ask himself if he is noble or if he is striving to be noble. It is inexcusable for parents not to ask themselves these questions when they think of the activity of the life force in their children. If the children are near a truly great person, they are undaunted by him, and the unhampered life force in children will internalize that person's nobleness in such a way that they could be said to soak it up.

When I think of these things, I know that we must study much more both for our sakes and for the sake of our children.

A Child of Any Race Can Develop

Ability can be developed in children of any race.

In the future there will come a time when man will not ask what race a child is, but will think of humanity as a whole. I believe that the foolish parts of human history were often due to racial prejudice.

The Western world had the preconceived idea that Japanese people did not know Western music and performed it without sensitivity. Yet Japan successfully produced excellent musicians. When I lectured in America, I asked the audience when I had finished, "Japanese people are known for being unmusical. What do you think?"

"Certainly it was true thirty or forty years ago, but after listening to your lecture we know that saying that is a mistake. Now we cannot say that it is true," was the answer. This is the result of making Kreisler, Casals, and the greatest musicians in the world the teachers of sensitivity for thirty years. This sensitivity was internalized by small children.

Japanese musicians have appeared all over the world to take the entrance exams to music schools, play in orchestras, and even become concertmasters. The Western music world was surprised that the Japanese people could show such musicality so suddenly.

Ivan Galamian of the Juilliard School* wrote in a magazine, "For a long century the Jewish people have been the principals in the violin world. However, it may be that Asian people will be the principal violinists, now." There is fact behind those words. Kenji Kobayashi and many other students of mine have studied under Galamian. He compared them with his American and European students and felt that they were highly sensitive.

A child who is raised in the best possible environment from early childhood will internalize a high level of sensitivity, enough to be admired even by Galamian. The child accomplishes this in the same way that a child in Osaka learns the Osaka dialect. Using this method only for music would be regrettable when it can be adapted to any area.

*A highly respected music conservatory in New York.

Not Only Gifted Children Can Develop

Any child can develop in any way. I was very disappointed in the way the newspapers reported the concerts of Toshiya Eto or Koji Toyoda. I was interviewed by the newspapers after each concert. I specifically said, "Do not call them geniuses. Any child can do the same if he is taught according to the principles of Talent Education." In spite of what I told them, the morning paper of the next day had, "Genius is Revealed" in large print. I was shocked.

It certainly was a wonderful thing that little Toshiya and Koji could develop so much. If they are child geniuses, then it is no longer amazing.

Then I thought of a good idea. I decided to have thousands of children play in concert with their *genius*. The performance that had been termed *genius* a long time ago is now performed by hundreds of children in groups.

Chapter 3

A Prayerful Heart Is the Spirit Which Should Nurture Children

This Era Is Not Yet Civilized

As we approach the twenty-first century, humans in the world are not yet civilized. Man has been fighting continuously since the stone age when he used sticks and stones. Our wisdom has not grown. We have only progressed from sticks and stones to swords, guns, and bigger guns, to atomic and hydrogen bombs. The fundamental aim to kill each other has not changed. I cannot say that this is a very civilized age.

We must reflect upon the twentieth century and make the twenty-first century civilized. This is our mission. Convenience is fine, but we are not civilized when we make killing convenient. There is no direct connection between convenience and happiness.

Children are the foundation of an era. We need all parents to be determined to raise their children as truly civilized human beings. A truly civilized human being is thoughtful of others, pours his love on others, knows the joy of living, and enjoys working for the happiness of all. Such a person loves other people and other people love him in return. Raising children to become such people is the best gift we can give them, and it will help in civilizing this world.

Prayer Is in the Heart of a Parent

At least once, every mother has held her baby and prayed that her child will be happy and healthy for all of his life. However, when the baby becomes five or six years old his mother complains that he is disobedient and a problem. Then, having become tired of the everyday problems, she may think at times, "My life would be easier without this child."

Somewhere near you there is a parent who continuously scolds her child and complains that he is unruly and disobedient, not realizing how inadequately she has raised her child.

I tell such parents, "Once a day go into a room alone and, remembering what you said to yourself when the child was a baby, again say, 'I hope that this child is happy and healthy all of his life.' It only takes ten seconds to say this little prayer. Then leave the room and look at the face of your child again. It will seem to have changed."

A prayer is when you whisper the hopes of your heart. After listening to that hope and leaving the room you will not feel like scolding your children anymore. Your child will respond with a happy face when he looks at your motherly one.

The real heart of a parent is prayerful. Today it is easy to forget the prayerful heart and to settle for resentfulness and rebukes.

Reflect Upon the Home Environment

The word *reflect* is easily misunderstood. If I tell people to *reflect*, I sound like a restrained ethics teacher.

Reflection is a wonderful human ability. It is the ability to understand faults and pursue the correct way. People who contemplate their faults tend to be more humane, and those who contemplate deeply are very great.

A parent who understands that children grow by adapting to their environment will think back on his own actions when he notices something in his child that is not good. This is because he knows that the child has absorbed the actions of his parent. A parent who reflects in this way possesses an admirable heart.

Suppose a father opens the door with his foot. The next day his child copies him and does the same thing. The mother sees the child and scolds him. The child would never have thought of opening the door with his foot by himself. He copied an adult. He absorbed the action of his father. If this is noticed, it can be seen that children do what their parents do. If the parent changes, the child also will change unconsciously. When a person reflects, he opens his eyes to truth. Parents who do not reflect in this way are merely training their children as they would farm animals.

Parents who wish to raise noble children should get rid of their own problems by self-reflection. Then the entire household will be brighter and the children will grow up in a pleasant atmosphere. Parents should not argue in front of their children, because the children will absorb every slight nuance of the argument due to their sensitivity.

Koji Toyoda

I went to Kiso Fukushima during the war. Koji Toyoda had been my student in Tokyo but the war separated us. I heard rumors of his father dying in a car accident after he was drafted for work in a factory. The mother of Koji had died of illness. Having heard the rumor of Koji being orphaned, I was shocked.

I immediately contacted the NHK, Japan National Broadcasting Co., "People Search" program and asked for the whereabouts of Koji Toyoda to be reported to me in Kiso Fukushima. A month later I learned that Koji was living with his uncle in Hamamatsu helping out in an Oden shop.* I wrote a letter to his uncle saying that I wanted to see Koji.

Koji and his parents had moved to Tokyo from Hamamatsu and he had become my student because his parents wanted him to become a fine artist and person. I decided to become his foster parent so that their efforts would not be wasted. Koji was brought to Kiso Fukushima by his uncle.

At that time my aunt, my younger sister, and her two children were in Kiso Fukushima. We rented the second floor of a house and Koji came to live with us. Unfortunately, Koji had learned some bad habits with little etiquette during the three years since his parents died. My sister's two children picked up his bad habits. Koji was thought to have a bad influence upon them.

Then I called a family meeting while the children were at school. I said, "Koji picked up his bad habits naturally while living in Hamamatsu. It is not his fault. If everyone complains about him, he will only think, 'It is because I am not a member of this family.' That would not be good for Koji. We should live an orderly and clean life ourselves before we grumble about him."

Everyone listened to my proposal willingly. We all started being careful of our good manners, even to the extent of exchanging greetings and lining up the shoes whenever entering the house. We were silent and did not complain. We took care to change our own actions and have a proper attitude towards life.

Year by year, Koji adapted to his new environment. Eventually his lifestyle matched our own. He naturally

*A small food store.

and unconsciously changed so that he did everything properly without having been scolded at all.

If everyone had tried to correct Koji by scolding him, he would have thought it was because he was not part of the family. If Koji began to feel this way it would be inexcusable on our part to both Koji and his parents who loved him. It was much better for us to correct our own lives.

Scolding children without changing oneself does not help the children. "Being good" is in their minds, but their actions come from their life force. The life force is stronger. Even if a child tries to be good, his life force has adapted to his environment and he will continue to do what he always has done. For the same reason, it is difficult for a person to stop speaking Osaka dialect when everyone around him is speaking it. The best method is to go to a place where no one speaks the Osaka dialect. *Man is the son of his environment* is something that I always write. It is the basis of my philosophy. A *problem* child comes from a *problem* parent.

The Child and the Storehouse

About fourteen or fifteen years ago, I lectured in Kicho in Aichi Prefecture. There I spoke about my pet theory that children develop through environmental adaptation.

"Saying that a child was *born* obstinate is incorrect. He has lived every day being scolded and so his ability to scold was developed. Look at the poor, miserable form of your child. That is the way you brought him up to be," I said. Everyone seemed to be impressed.

That night I stayed at the house of a company president. The next morning while his wife was serving breakfast to me she said, "Mr. Suzuki, I have an embarrassing confession to make." Then she told the following story:

"I often become angry with my child because he is very disobedient and sassy. I pulled him to the small outside storage building thinking I would shut him in as I always do. As I opened the door to push him in, I could hear your words, 'That is the way you brought him up to be.' I held my child and we went into the storage building together. After closing the door I apologized to him saying, 'It is my fault that you are so disobedient. I am going to try to be a better mother for you. Please forgive me. As a part of that promise, I will stay in the storehouse with you.'"

" 'That's not so. I am bad. Really I am the one who is bad,' cried my child and he clung to me. Finally the two of us cried together in the storehouse."

"This morning, what did the face of your child look like?" I asked.

"My child had a tender and calm expression on his face," she answered.

"You also have a tender expression on your face," I said. "Your relationship will become closer from now on I am sure."

This mother not only reflected on what she had done, but put the results into action.

The Masseuse

The following incident happened about two years ago when I went to Tokyo. Upon arrival at my hotel, I asked for a massage because I was very tired. The masseuse was about 35 years old and she talked to me as she worked.

"Saying that a child is a blessing is very true. Having a good child or a bad child gives a parent good or bad luck. I am very unlucky because my child is unspeakably bad." Hearing this I could not help but tell her about Talent Education.

"That is the way you brought him up to be," I said. Gradually she stopped massaging and started crying.

"Why are you crying?" I asked.

"I must be a very bad parent. I started crying when I thought of all the dreadful things I have done to that poor child. I cannot continue this massage."

"Your reflection will make you a better mother and your child will become happy. Look at your child tonight with the heartfelt feeling that your actions have been unpardonable. Words are unnecessary. The feeling is enough," I said.

"If that is true then I must try it, I promise you," she said and we parted that night.

A month and a half later I was back in Tokyo for the Talent Education National Concert. After the concert I was tired and again asked for a massage at my hotel. By chance, the same lady of a month and a half earlier came.

"I had been wanting to find you and say thank you. Now I have that chance," she said, and upon inquiry she continued. "A miraculous thing happened. I looked at my child with the feeling of being unpardonable. I said nothing to him, but recently he has changed and become a very good child. When I am working he says, 'Mother, let me help you.' Our fights have ceased. Thank you very much." She looked very happy.

"Your child will surely become a fine person," I said, and we parted. It was very admirable that the mother could be apologetic to her child. This is necessary if we are to become more civilized.

Chapter 4

Parents Are Haughty

Do Not Show Favoritism

Parents are unconsciously haughty towards their children. The main reason for this is that the mother thinks her child belongs to her. A mother is subconsciously under the illusion that the life she bore is her possession. A mother remembers changing diapers, pulling legs, turning the child over, holding him, putting him to sleep and generally following her own will when the child was a baby. These memories affect a mother so that eventually she thinks that the child will do as she expects.

When a child becomes four or five years old and is disobedient, his mother becomes overly angry because he no longer follows her every wish. The haughty, or arrogant heart of a parent now begins to develop unconsciously. All parents have this feeling to a greater or lesser degree and can interact better with their children only after self-reflection.

I often tell parents that they are much too demanding towards their own children. The facial expressions of a mother are greatly different when dealing with someone else's child. A mother faced with her own child's disobedience thinks that she will make him obey, and her face becomes stern. Often what would be a simple request is replaced by a command. Yet, if the same mother wants the same action from another's child, she will ask that child nicely. Of course the child is happy to comply.

All children have the same, wonderful life force. If a parent is pleasant and nice toward other children and stern with his own, then the parent-child relationship will not be good. Parents should use the same pleasant facial expressions with their own children as they use with other children. It means respecting human life. Even the life of a small child requires respect.

It is easy for parents to make this language distinction between siblings, also. Dr. Kaname Hori, a psychiatrist and a director of Talent Education, often speaks on this subject.

When Dr. Hori was a child, his younger brother tended to be disobedient. Their mother would say to the eldest, "Take a bath while the water is hot," and he would do so, feeling obedient. To his younger brother, however, she would say, "The water is hot so hurry up and take a bath, or else!" At that time she would use a harsh voice. The younger brother was repulsed by her tone of voice and disobeyed. Because the parent classified one brother as obedient and the other as disobedient, she would use pleasant language to the one and harsh language to the other.

If a parent spoke pleasantly to all children, he would be sure to raise brighter and more obedient children. Parents should reflect upon their arrogance.

Do Not Cheat Yourself

Education has been given various definitions, but I would define it as knowledge of and respect for the nobleness of human beings. An education which consists primarily of following orders creates bad results.

When I was seventeen I was very impressed with Tolstoy. I was especially impressed by the words, "Do not cheat yourself." Tolstoy wrote in his diary that it is worse to cheat yourself than to cheat another. I thought that I wanted to learn fror.. children and their natural life force. I then studied small children as examples.

Small children soon become friends with me. Not only in Japan, but also at lectures and institutes in America, many children three, four, and five years old gather around me. A while ago a three-year-old child gave me two old flashcubes. It seemed as if they were a present from him so I said, "Thank you," and took him to his mother. I asked her what the child was saying.

"He says that he gave Mr. Suzuki his treasure because he likes Mr. Suzuki," she answered. It makes me very happy that a child I had never talked to before would give me his treasure. Many people in America have said that children like me so much because I love them. I answered, "Everyone loves children. I *respect* children as my teachers."

I am often misunderstood and some people even make faces, but it is possible that the children come to me because I radiate respect for them.

Love can be given to cats and dogs because they are cute, but we should not love children for that reason alone. We should love children for the pure, beautiful things that radiate from their hearts. *Love* and *respect* combined is what establishes a bond.

A Caress From a Ragamuffin

There was a big kindergarten meeting in Suwa City in Nagano prefecture. I and other lecturers spoke to a gathering of kindergarten and nursery school principals and teachers.

That evening after the meeting, I was sitting on a bench in Suwa Station. Many kindergarten teachers were waiting with me for the train. Suddenly, from behind, a child gently rubbed his cheek against mine. I had him come to me. As he got near he suddenly jumped away again, and he hugged me and rubbed his cheek against mine from behind once more. His face was red, his clothes were in rags, and he was barefoot. I asked him to come so that I could hold him. Again he approached, but suddenly he ran away and again rubbed his cheek against mine from behind.

Just then a man who could have been his father appeared from the far exit. The man also had unkempt hair and wore rags. He yelled to the child who gave a startled jump and ran towards him.

It made me happy that the child felt the radiation of my human sensitivity even though from behind. The sensitivity of that child and the willingness to caress me even from behind moved me very deeply.

The Heart Radiates

I was lecturing at a small kindergarten in the Kansai Area. After the lecture I sat in the middle of the front row in the room while listening to the children give a concert. Just then a barefooted beggar child of six or seven came to my side and confronted me. I invited him to sit in the empty seat next to me so that we could listen together. The child nodded in acceptance and listened quietly.

At the end of one piece I clapped and said to the child, "Good, aren't they?" The child clapped too and returned my smile with a laugh. He listened to the next piece quietly, also. I asked him if it was interesting and he said, while he clapped, that it was very interesting.

After the concert ended, the kindergarten teachers expressed surprise. That child, who often sneaked into the kindergarten to play with the children, was the child of a wandering tramp. The word spread. "That child cannot settle down. He cannot concentrate upon one thing. He often gets in the way so I have to put him out. What could have happened today?"

"I saw the child sit right next to Mr. Suzuki and he sat down until the end. He even clapped his hands."

It was not miraculous. The child could feel my radiations of respect for children, and when I spoke to him with praise and interest, he was happy to be treated as an equal human being. The attitude of the child changed because of the way in which he was treated changed. Instead of being treated as a pest, he was treated as an equal. It was easy for the child to sit for an hour because it was fun.

The heart radiations, and the thoughts and feelings of a person, show all over. The ragamuffin in Suwa probably had no mother. He had only a barefoot tramp in rags. Even a child of such an environment could feel the wonderfulness of human life. A child has so much ability.

Reverence for children is reverence for life.

The Heart That Feels Music Will Feel People

I think that music is the most wonderful one of the man-made arts. If we listen to the music of Bach or Mozart, we can feel the hearts of Bach and Mozart in their music. Maybe at first only the melody is understood, but after continuous listening it is possible to understand all of the religious, sensitive, overpowering personality of Bach. With Mozart, his loving personality is packed into his music. Even now, Bach and Mozart live in their works. This is the beauty and wonder of music.

If a child is raised on Bach from a young age, the noble soul, the powerful personality and the religious sensitivity of Bach will develop in the child. If a child is raised on Mozart, then the loving soul of Mozart will develop in the child. The life force in the child will absorb those traits to a high level. The heart that feels music will feel people.

ment to America while he was a student of Oberlin
College. He said that Mr. Stokowski would like to meet
me.

Leopold Stokowski is a world famous conductor. We
contacted him and arranged a visit. This wonderful musician was already eight-six or eighty-seven years old. He
had shining white hair and met me with a smile. After
the usual small talk, he asked me if I would listen to his
philosophy of life.

"My philosophy is not to hurt anyone, therefore not
hurting my own heart," he said quietly.

Do not hurt anyone else and do not hurt your own
heart. I was moved. If one person hurts another, he hurts
himself as well. These words contained a great spirit and
sincere love. This is how Stokowski could be such a great
musician.

The music is the man.

There Are No Two People Exactly Alike

Since I often assert that *talent is not inborn* and
every child develops, many people misunderstand me and
ask if there is not superior or inferior inborn talent. I have
never said that the inborn ability of children is the same.
There are no two people exactly alike. However, superior
or inferior ability at birth cannot be judged from the
eventual results.

A difference in ability will show when we look at
the results. However, it cannot be said that this difference
is inborn. Results come from an intertwining of factors
such as the environment and the learning situation. If we
look only at the results, then the lowest human beings born
today have greater ability than those born in the Stone
Age. An excellent inborn ability to have is the ability to
learn. I would like to know the possibilities of a baby.

As an example, suppose that three newborn babies
were taken to Alaska. The three babies will adapt in dif-

ferent fashions. I will call the children *A, B,* and *C. A* quickly adapts to the cold and is very healthy, catching no colds. *B* constantly catches colds with fever. After about three years, he finally adapts to the cold. *C* also continuously catches cold, and eventually catches pneumonia and dies.

Of these three children, *A* has the superior inborn ability to adapt, *B* is next, and *C* has inferior ability. It is the speed and sensitivity with which a baby adapts to his environment that creates ability. Superior or inferior ability is dependent upon the life force of a child. A baby will grow up in the way he is reared. He has the possibility of becoming a great person. Do not give up on a child and decide he was a born failure.

The consideration that all healthy children speak their own language indicates that every child can be educated. Therefore, the ability to become well educated and a great person is shown to exist in anyone who has developed an ability in language.

Chapter 5

The Making of a Person

Anger Is Unnecessary in Everyday Life

I have often talked about not scolding children, and I would like to expand more fully upon the relationship between anger and ability.

There are some people whose only ability is to display anger and their facial expression always looks angry. Such people may start by becoming angry only occasionally, but eventually as they scold more often it becomes a habit to be angry. The habitually angry person is a veteran scolder and his face colors with anger at the smallest things. What an unhappy person.

I have reflected upon anger and concluded that anger is unnecessary in human life. Practice not being angry instead of developing an ability for anger. I myself practiced not becoming angry for ten years. It changed me from my very roots. What experiences I had!

One day a person challenged me with a knotty problem. He also said some terrible things while my colleagues were in the next room. As I listened to him, I thought that a person capable of saying such things without reason must have grown up in a poor environment. Then instead of feeling anger, I felt sympathy. As his anger progressed, he exposed his poor development and I felt no anger at all. Therefore, I could answer him with kind words of sympathy. Harsh words do not require more harsh words.

My colleagues in the next room were irritated and became very angry. They told me they felt like shaking their fists at him, and wanted to know how I could speak to him so easily. They felt that it was necessary to scold such people or subsequently I would be despised.

I answered, "When I remember that such people must come from unhappy situations, I cannot be angry. It is unnecessary for me to enter the same miserable situation to fight with him."

I can become angry, but I have stopped doing so. My ability to show sympathy has become stronger than my ability to display anger. With only that one change, my life has settled down and meeting people has become pleasant. If I do not scold another, he will not be able to scold me. Then we can be pleasant and amiable.

"I am Hans Von Bülow"

I volunteered to be an interviewing committeeman of the Matsumoto juvenile prison. I often had the chance to go to the prison to encourage the youths to discard their inferiority complexes and recognize themselves as fine human beings.

"Regardless of the crime, each of you did a terrible thing. You may have the misconception that to be a strong person you should often become very angry. But you must work to lessen the anger in life. Please practice not getting angry."

Then I would tell them the story of Hans Von Bülow. Hans Von Bülow was a friend of Brahms. These days he is a great conductor in Europe. He has a very humorous spirit and has left us with many humorous stories.

One day Hans was running down the stairs of his hotel for an urgent appointment. At the same time, another man was running up the stairs and they bumped into each other. The man shouted, "Stupid idiot!"

Then Hans said pleasantly, "How do you do? I am Hans Von Bülow."

It is the custom in Germany to greet another person by introducing oneself. If I were to greet someone, I would say, "I am Mr. Suzuki. How do you do?"

Therefore, when Hans answered the shout with a greeting and self introduction, the words said by the other man changed to mean, "I am Stupid Idiot." This is a humorous and wonderful moment in which Hans turned another's sword back the other way through the use of humor.

After telling the story I suggested that the youths try the same technique. If another person is enough of a stupid idiot to say, "Stupid Idiot!," it is unnecessary to become angry. It is enough to think that the person introduced himself as Stupid Idiot and return the introduction. Then there will be no argument.

We then started keeping a record of how often each youth became angry. The next month, various things like "Raged with anger," "Became angry but controlled himself," and "Became angry but made up immediately" were recorded on the chart. At that time, "Became angry but controlled himself" and better marks like "Did not become angry" were about twenty-five percent. However, in the following month, the "Did not become angry" score went up over seventy percent.

Keeping such detailed statistics for themselves resulted in the practice of not becoming angry. The atmosphere was completely changed. The facial expressions of the youths became more amiable. This result made me happy.

The "Not Angry" Game

Make a game of not becoming angry at home. Every home has a calendar. Put an *Anger Graph* near it. It is best if the entire family keeps a record. A record is kept of how many times each becomes angry every day, and a total is made for each month. While keeping such records, maybe a time will come in which no one becomes angry at all for the entire month.

As a person learns not to become angry, his heart becomes more amiable and he becomes better at helping others. At the same time he will become able to live without pestering his companions by polluting the air with his anger. Please play the *Not Angry game*. Even if it starts as only a game, you will find that injurious anger will naturally become extinguished.

A child who is raised by a short tempered parent develops a short temper like his parent. He will become enraged at his friends without cause. His ability for anger has been trained every day through the educational method of his parents. Anger is the ability to become angry.

Make an *Anger Graph* and gradually you will lose the ability to become angry as you fill in the graph every day. The number of times you become angry will naturally lessen and you will become kinder to others. Then the household atmosphere will become more bright and pleasant.

There are people who are full of smiles in public, but are carelessly angry in their homes. This should not happen. People must respect the feelings of others and treasure the person to person relationship within the home as well as without.

I often hear stories of fathers who smile as they leave the front door and who are amiable, good people at work, but become very angry when they come home with no consideration for those around them. There are many people who defend such fathers saying that after a day of patience and smiles they cannot help but vent their anger at home. This is a mistake.

Such a person must be regarded as one who fell into the habit of being selfish and angry at home. He should be the same inside and outside of the house. A man should not find fault with his wife because she is his wife. Respect as human beings as well as trusting love are necessary between a husband and wife, also.

Anger causes much stress. Laughing and dissolving the stress at home is a better provision for tomorrow than building up stress through needless anger.

Do Not Rely on General Assumptions

For a long time I have explained that anger is unnecessary in child education. Now we must consider *general assumptions* in relation to ability development.

When we rely on general assumptions, it is normal for us not to use anything but that. However, a common assumption is what someone in the past decided was true and that we take for granted. We should examine these things at least once. There could be an error.

People often say, "I was born to mediocrity," or "Surely I am no genius," and other things about inborn talent. Now everyone understands that this assumption is in error. We must recognize that we were born as wonderful human beings with limitless possibilities.

A person is not born uninteresting. He is trained to be ordinary. When the majority of people are right-handed, left-handed people are considered almost abnormal. However, if left-handed people are abnormal, then right-handed people should also be considered abnormal. When I went to the zoo, I found that monkeys function in a better way. They are ambidextrous. We have made an error in our assumptions.

Right-Handedness, Left-Handedness

I am right-handed. When I was young, I was the shortstop on a baseball team, and therefore can throw quite well. I would hold the ball in my right hand and I could throw it accurately far enough to feel pleased. My left hand could throw the ball only a third of the distance and the aim was inaccurate. Both hands belong to the same human being and the left hand is the same as the right, but my left hand is like that of a retarded child.

There is a closed relationship between training and human development. If both of my hands were like my left hand, I would not be able to do anything. Such a big difference between the left and right hands of the same person is like the difference between an educated and an uneducated person.

Being Ambidextrous Is Ideal

I think that raising children to be ambidextrous would be best. It is preferable to be able to use both hands freely.

I know one lady who is ambidextrous. When she does needlework she sews from the right until she tires and then she sews from the left. She can even cut radishes into long, thin pieces freely from either left or right. If parents could raise their children to be ambidextrous it would be very handy and efficient.

Suppose each hand was a child. One handed is like educating one child and ignoring the other. If raising a child to be left-handed is unfair, then raising a child to be right-handed is also unfair.

Because in our environment the majority of things are made for right-handed people, we become more and more right-handed. This also is because of what I would call an error in common assumption which says that humans are right-handed, and as a result most things are made for right-handed people.

If one raised a child to be ambidextrous, how happy that child would be.

Even for practicing the piano, I think that what is necessary is to train the left hand for an extended number of hours so that both left and right hands can play with the same power. Thus a wonderful pianist will be created when even the left hand can play the piano as well as the right.

Do not rely on common suppositions. The reason I have spoken so much about left-handed and right-handed is because I think that by looking at something from a new angle, one can have the excitement of discovery and of grasping a new truth.

Personality Is a Talent

Developing one's personality is talked about as if it were an obvious result of education. The problem is that parents and teachers call what is a well developed ability in a child his personality.

Behind *personality development* lies hidden the easy way of educating a child. The child is being educated in something he has already been trained to do well. Then people mistakenly call that ability an inborn ability, and make another error by assuming this.

Last year, sixty university professors came to the Matsumoto Talent Education Research Center. We had a discussion hour in the auditorium. One teacher bega⁻ by asking for my thoughts on personality. I answered bv asking what was meant by *personality*. Everyone startea laughing because they thought that I did not understand the *word*. Then I continued:

"I wonder if trained ability is often mistaken for personality. When people talk about personality, it seems that they are talking about the most well trained ability in the child rather than his personality. Such an ability is not the inborn individuality of the child. If people want to stress having a strong personality, then they should raise children to develop such an admirable personality."

Develop Only Wonderful Characteristics

When people talk about developing personality, regardless of other factors, there are problems. Suppose the child of a pickpocket was good at stealing things. There would be a problem with expanding such a personality under the present definition. It is necessary to raise a child with more desirable characteristics. It is easier to understand if we realize that being an individual constitutes developing an ability. Then we can develop excellent abilities instead of merely expanding an existing personality.

If an ability the child has developed is a good one, then of course it would be good to expand it. However, if an ability the child has developed is not so admirable, like stealing, then it is better not to expand it, but to develop other abilities instead.

British people have their own individual characteristics. That is because they were born and raised in Britain. If a British child were brought to Japan at the time of birth and raised by a Japanese parent, then he would not have British-like characteristics. Individuality is an ability, and that child would have Japanese-like characteristics. His body would be that of a Briton, but his actions would have Japanese characteristics.

The foundation of education is to carefully raise children with the ability to be fine human beings without being hindered by their individual characteristics.

Teachers, Have Pride

The frustration of a school teacher is great. It is a terrible situation to have poorly raised children, undeveloped children, children who have been ignored and have become nearly retarded, and well reared children with excellent ability, all together in the same classroom. School teachers are under much strain. They use much effort with little fruition. We must have respect for their behavior.

At the same time, I think that the state should choose people who are worthy of respect to be teachers, and then give them a worthy income. If the present day teachers are superior people, then we can have wonderful dreams for the future of education.

Teachers should have more pride in what they do. In Japan, elementary and junior high schools are like preparatory factories for high school, and high school is like a preparatory factory for the university. Too much emphasis is put on the qualifying entrance exams. Teachers have lost their pride in shaping the adults of tomorrow.

Experienced Teachers Are Necessary

Experienced teachers are needed in elementary and junior high schools. The university is where adults investigate learning, but elementary and junior high schools have the responsibility of developing human beings.

I would like to see private citizens enter the ranks of elementary and junior high school teachers. People who have retired and who were respected as good people would be excellent teachers. They could be recommended by the city or by another person, or they could be interviewed. Developing the adults of tomorrow is an important job. Help would be welcomed from such experienced people.

Chapter 6

The Fate of a Child Is In the Hands of His Parents

From the Day of Birth

"When is a good time to start the violin?"

"My child is three years old. Is that too early to start the piano?"

I am frequently asked such inappropriate questions. It has often been said that it is best to start lessons from such-and-such an age, or starting too early is damaging. These opinions are erroneous. They are only theories. Can you conceive of thinking, "It is best to teach my child how to speak when he is five years old. Therefore he should not hear anyone speak until then." Nonsense! If a person actually did that to a child, it would be far too late for learning the language.

I do not think that anyone will ever find any bad effects from teaching a child his language at such an early age that he speaks fluently by the time he is five. The problem arises when the child is ignored during these important years.

From the day of birth, the body gradually grows, and the child adapts to his environment. When cultivating plants, it is obvious that a seedling will wither if it is assumed that no water, sunshine, or fertilizer should be given to the plant until a specific time, and then it is flooded with all three. Humans also exist within the realm of nature. In principle, we are no different than plants.

The Words of Darwin

There was a conversation between Darwin and a mother:

"From what age is it best to educate a child?"

"How old is your child?"

"My child is a year and a half."

"Then you are a year and a half late."

He made it clear that birth is the best time to start. For musical ability, play the most beautiful music on records from the day of birth. We develop to different forms dependent upon our environment. A child in an environment full of laughter will be full of charm and bright laughter. A child in an environment where nobody laughs will be unable to laugh and will be cold and sulky.

Beginning later is too late. A parent must remember about the life force of the baby and raise the child happily. The earlier talent development is begun, the better.

I am an unsuitable example for Talent Education children in the area of left hand, little finger training. I started practicing the violin formally when I was twenty-one. Therefore the little finger of my left hand will not move because I have not used it. Even if I merely try hitting the string with each finger several times, my little finger moves slowly and weakly compared to the other fingers. I had to train that finger fifty to a hundred times more than the other fingers. This training required much effort.

If a three year old child starts practicing the violin, his little finger will be as strong and agile as his other fingers. He will be able to do splendid fourth finger trills. Such a small child may only need to train a thousand times while an adult will not be able to achieve such skill after training even one hundred fifty thousand times.

I am not saying that an adult cannot learn. Only that an adult needs much more training than a small child does to reach the same level of ability. We are amazed at the wonders of early development of ability.

"The child at three learns more easily than the adult of one hundred."

The same can be said about the teaching of etiquette. Children behave the same as their parents. They absorb the actions of their parents by merely watching their parents. This is the same whether they are scolded or not. Children only know the way their parents act, and so they act accordingly. Small children do not learn by will power, they learn as a natural function of growth.

The Fate of a Child . . .

"The fate of a child is in the hands of the parent."

Shaping a child into an admirable human being or a wolf* is entirely dependent upon the parent. I teased a women's club in Kyoto by saying, "There are many parents in this world who are half wolf. Their children will grow up to be people with terrible attitudes in their hearts. The children have been ignored and their talent is lost. There are many such children who have lost the time for developing talent."

The majority of the members at the meeting began to cry. The president of the club said, "We, the half-wolf parents, would like to thank you . . ." through her tears. I was at a loss, so I apologized.

Everyone had heard my words as though they were an arrow of truth piercing deep into their hearts.

---

*A reference to human babies reportedly raised by wolves and displaying animal behavior.

Hold Them and Love Them

The love a parent feels for his children is the kind of love that appeals to life. Children sense our expressions strongly.

There is a big difference between the baby who was breast-fed and the baby who was separated from his mother and bottle-fed. It is unfortunate for the separated and bottle-fed baby that the bond with his mother is weak. There is nothing as good as mother's milk, and love between parent and child exists when the lives are tied together through the giving and receiving of milk. Science talks about nourishment and calories as if raising human children were the same as raising cattle.

Frederich II of Germany conducted a bold experiment. He wondered what language a baby would speak if no language was taught to him. He thought that if children were not taught, maybe they would speak old Hebrew. He gathered many abandoned children and put all the babies in one room. He hired nurses to nourish them. For his experimental purposes, the nourishment was given without saying a word or holding the children. No Hebrew emerged and no child spoke any language. The children, who had not been held, had weak life forces and died quickly.

It is difficult for life to exist without love.

To Succeed or Not Succeed

People often talk about whether a child will become a success or not. Unfortunately the heart of the question involves ability. Using the ability or inability to earn money as a measure of whether a child will become great or not is like saying that humans were born with the sole purpose of being able to make a living.

One of my students was brought up well. He studied earnestly and he played the violin well. One day his mother asked me, "Will my child become something?"

"No, he will not," I answered quietly. She was shocked, so I continued, "Are you thinking that you will not allow your child to play the violin if he is not going to become something through it?" Often I am repelled when a parent asks me that question because I feel her calculating whether or not the child can support himself by his musical ability. I said, "Your child is well brought up and he has a fine artistic sense. By never becoming a success, he will become a wonderful person. I did not mean that he has no promise for development. He is being well brought up. It is unfair to him to use words that imply being mercenary." Now she understood well.

If a parent can raise a child to be a talented, admirable person, that is enough. Later, the child himself will make his own way. If a child is brought up to have a beautiful heart and wonderful abilities, with love for others and the happiness of being loved, then the mission of a parent is ended. The way will open up for the child later. Parents do not need to worry whether or not their children will succeed.

My Father's Words

There is one memory of my youth which I cannot forget. One night my father asked me, "What are you praying for every night when you go to the shrine?"

"I pray, 'Please keep my home safe and healthy. I leave my future up to you,' " I answered.

My father smiled bitterly and said, "From today on, stop speaking like an insect. It is enough to pray, 'Thank you very much,' but do not ask for your wants."

I remember my father fondly when I think about raising people who can always feel thankful instead of always wanting something. He taught me to open doors by myself instead of asking others to open them for me.

Exceptional Talent, Exceptional Heart

Here is an episode that happened when I was teaching at the Imperial School of Music in Tokyo.

Everyone in my class practiced hard and came to perform very well. One Yamamoto, who had taken first place in an NHK competition, also came to the class. Every day we had a lesson.

One very cold and wintry morning, the stove in the room was burning well. Before the students came, I opened the end window half way. Then I went to the faculty room, watched the time, and entered the classroom with the students.

We were about to start the lesson when Yamamoto jumped up and closed the window. Then I said to the class, "Actually, I am the one who had opened that window. I went back again to the faculty room, and re-entered the classroom and sat down with everyone else. However, out of all of you, only Yamamoto noticed the open window and closed it. The others sat silently waiting for my lesson. Everyone knows that Yamamoto took first place in the competition. He truly uses his head. Not only is his violin technique good, but he noticed that the window was open on such a cold day when he entered the room, and he went and closed it for everyone. Having great ability means having a deep and great ability of the heart. If you would like to make yourselves more talented, then you should make your hearts more talented. When you see scraps of paper on the floor, if you have the talent to put them in a wastebasket, your performance also should become more delicately beautiful. This talk is today's lesson."

From much experience, I can clearly state that truly great talent customarily accompanies a beautiful and deep heart.

Another time, when I heard one student play the violin, although the performance was good, I felt that there was something egotistical in the student's playing. Therefore, after listening I said, "Stop playing the violin for a week. There is something you must learn besides the violin. It is the spirit of doing things for other people. Practice this work for one week. To begin with, pick up your friend's books when they have fallen on the floor, or put your friend's shoes neatly together when they have turned upside down, and if you are prepared to help all day, you will find many things to do. Live by looking for things to do for other people. This is your homework for the week."

Although the student said, "Yes, sir," and went home, he came to the faculty room after one week and asked, "Sir, what does doing things for other people have to do with violin practice? I do not really understand what you said, so I came to ask you again."

"When listening to your performance, I could clearly feel that you were self-centered in your heart. Therefore, I felt that your performance was narrow. If your heart is set to work for others, then your mind should be able to work more sensitively in an expanded world. If you do so, then more abundant, delicately beautiful expressions will enter your performance. Well, even if you think you were tricked, go and do your homework for another week."

That student eventually came to perform very beautifully.

I am always saying that art becomes higher as humans develop higher. Also, if everyone would study art, then art would come into everyday life. I hope that you can now understand that great talent and a deep, beautiful feeling in the heart are closely tied together.

Chapter 7

Talent and Love

Music Will Save the World

In 1961 I invited Pablo Casals, the great cellist, to Tokyo. Four hundred children performed to welcome him. When little children of five and six played concertos by Vivaldi and Bach, Casals was very moved. He hugged me with tears in his eyes, went up on the stage, and gave a wonderful speech. That speech started with "Music is not just sound." He also said, "Maybe music will save the world." The words, "Music will save the world," are held deep in my heart.

Recently I went to America, and when I lectured to university professors, I borrowed those words of Casals and used them in the same way that he did. However, I added something. "Maybe music will save the world. That is, if we work for that purpose," I said, and then continued, "There are people who think that art exists for its own sake, but I do not think so. Art exists for the human species. I think that all of the people who love art, those who teach art, and all of you, should burn with the obligation to save the world. It is necessary to be concerned about the importance of educating a really beautiful human spirit." Everyone gave me a standing ovation.

Teaching intonation, and teaching technique will never be more than a method. We are burning with a deeper mission that we must do something for the future.

Everyone sympathized with me from their hearts. Every-one was moved by the words, *if we work hard, music can save the world.*

I often say the following to my students and their mothers: "We do not have to become professional musi-cians. It is enough to grow up playing the violin."

"If, as a person works at playing the violin well, he develops the talent to overcome any difficult problem by working, then the talent will be born to accomplish even the hardest problems easily. As a person practices the violin, he creates this talent."

Music exists for the purpose of growing an admirable heart.

The Real Meaning of Sophistication

There are many memories associated with the words that music exists to elevate the human race. They are memories that made me think of the relationship between science and man's nobility.

The following is an old story of about forty years ago:

I met various kinds of people when I was in Ger-many. The attitudes of university graduates were so dif-ferent that after having just been introduced, I would suddenly feel, oh, this person is a university graduate. This does not mean that they brag. From their manner of speaking and content of speech, to their little courtesies, one can feel a very true culture radiating from their very bodies. Therefore, with only a few words exchanged, one can clearly tell that a person is a university graduate.

German education is such that graduation from a university not only means that higher knowledge is acquired, but that the attitude of the heart toward every day life has been refined, and that the level of culture has been raised to overflowing. This is where I feel that German education is splendid.

I came to know various kinds of people and to have many acquaintances, and although each had his good points, the feelings of the university graduates are clearly different whether you refer to the content of their speech or to their manners. A real meaning of sophistication is to be sensitive to another person's feelings, and have respect for their point of view. That is what the university graduates have in Germany.

Because this happened more than forty years ago, I do not know if present day Germany is the same or not. However, I think that the same is probably also true today.

In Japan, how is it that elementary school, junior high school, and university graduates are all the same? I think that having taken the trouble to graduate from the university, a deeper kindness toward other people and in one's own action is needed in an interpersonal situation. Is the emphasis on factual learning and intellectual training producing these kinds of defects?

I feel that recent tendencies are to think too much about person-to-person relations based on personal profit. Instead, we need to have person-to-person relations within an atmosphere of mutual deep consideration of the other person.

In the university, it is also necessary for those who have studied higher learning to have this kind of heart.

Education Through Age Seventeen

Physiologically speaking, the brain finishes its development at seventeen or eighteen. Therefore, I think that university education through that age is enough. Of course, I am able to say this from experience also. If the conditions for growing ability are good, as it is in the world of music, one can arrive at the highest standards of the world at seventeen or eighteen years old.

Therefore, I think that plans should be made to change the educational system so that seventeen and eighteen year olds graduate from the university, and the university becomes required education. Even with this plan, they should be able to attain fine knowledge and real ability not inferior to present day university students. If this were possible, the responsibility of parents would be lighter personally and economically because instead of putting their children through university until they are twenty-four or twenty-five, their children will graduate at seventeen or eighteen and then enter society, which I think is a much better policy.

More importantly, people who have grown that much ability at seventeen or eighteen will have a very high ability for taking action. When they jump into a job as a member of society they can, with a little guidance, be people of great help, but those people who enter society at twenty-four or twenty-five have problems adjusting. In other words, the age of eighteen is the age in which the most self-development takes place. What a waste it is to spend that time period only studying for entrance exams.

Based on this pet theory, I have a dream of establishing an experimental school with some people who share the same theory. Then, if I could show successful results to the state, I would be very happy. For that purpose I must hold to my intention of living to age 110.

Look at Parents

The idea that man's development depends on his environment has been repeated constantly until now. Therefore, when deciding on a groom or a bride, be sure to go to the other's home to meet the father and mother. This is an important consideration which decides your fate. Looking at the household and what the parents are like is something that must be done to ascertain what your mate is truly like.

Before marriage, both parties show each other only their best sides. After marriage, the true character of the home environment in which each has been raised will show its face regardless. In order to know that true character, it is necessary to go to the other's house and meet the other's parents.

Let's condense this down to the matter of *love* and look again. Let's consider the conditions at home where attitudes are developed. When parents love their children to the extent of "spoiling" them, the child develops a strong desire to be "spoiled" even more. The child knows only that kind of "love," and takes it for granted, and his desire for it grows stronger and stronger.

Parents grow older and the last son or daughter marries and has a separate house of his or her own. As a parent, because I loved the child so much, I expect that I will be treasured when I go to my son's or daughter's house. Anticipating a joyous visit, I go to my son's or daughter's house.

However, a son or daughter who has grown nothing but the ability to be loved will selfishly want the parent to continue to bring gifts for his or her pleasure. Therefore, a parent will get a cold welcome since he has different plans. The ability was never developed in the child to love his parents and be as kind to them as they were to him.

The parents regret that their son is so cold or their daughter's love is so thin. Even parents can get angry saying, "After I loved you so much you are so ungrateful." But that is natural. The parents themselves dispensed that kind of education to the child.

Wiser parents would have opened their hearts more in the area of love when raising their children. For instance, heartfelt kindness and warmth without a front could be offered when guests come. Even when the guest leaves, let the child hear words of love about the guest like, "She was a nice old lady, wasn't she," and "That guest was a really kind-hearted person."

However, suppose the opposite was done and when the guest leaves the following sort of words are said:

"A guest came when we were busy. It couldn't be helped, so we just put anything out, even cold tea."

Within such living, a child is also present and is watching and listening to the attitude of the parent.

Of course, a child raised by such a parent will have a cold heart. The parents will eagerly anticipate seeing the grandchild's face and will go to the son's or daughter's place. But without saying why they came, they will be given cold tea and be driven away. The attitude which the parent took towards people when the child was small, will be shown towards the parent by the son or daughter in the same fashion. What the parent did will be returned to the parent.

The child raised in a house where the entire family warmly welcomes guests will naturally gain that warmth himself. A child who has learned the happiness of bestowing love on others from the attitude of his parents will have the happiness of bestowing love on his parents when they come to visit. The nuance of what I am saying may be somewhat different, but my point is the same as the old saying, "You reap what you sow." This means that a parent who is an egotist and lives by showing unkindness to others will receive the cold return of unkindness from his children.

I want to be sure that when I say to look at the other's parents before marriage, this includes all that I have spoken about.

The Interest on Love

If there were no cash principal, there would be no interest.

The same is true for love. If a person does not make an investment in love, then his mate will not return the interest of love.

Young people on the verge of marriage and young people who are just married are giving each other so much cash that they would die for each other. That is why a large amount of interest comes back from the mate. The couple lives happily in a world of love and are fulfilled.

However, if ten or fifteen years after marriage, both of them have exhausted their cash, then interest does not come back from the mate. At this time it is said that love is gone. Neither of them invest new cash, but they both moan that love has cooled off.

During the war, I was sent to Kiso Fukushima and worked as the manager of a plant cutting and preparing cypress for use in making planes. At that time, I gathered everyone at the plant everyday before work and played the violin to cleanse their hearts and make them feel fresh. Then I gave them a daily lesson.

At that time I often suggested things to make the home pleasant. "If, when you go home today, your wife has been preparing supper and waiting for you, think of this practice and say to her, 'You must be tired after waiting at home all day and then fixing supper for me. Thank you very much.' " If you feel shy, you can use a low voice. Your wife may be surprised and roll her eyes a little. Even so, never mind and try saying it once. Then she will come out of the kitchen carrying the plates. At that time, jump up and try saying 'I will carry the plates, also.'

"And then in the evening, when your wife goes to close the shutters, say 'I will help also,' and close half of them. The cash of love must be invested in the home. Even with such a little bit of cash, interest returns will soon come. To begin with, arguments will be cut in half and your wife will fix your meals with her heart in her work, which will surely make them taste better. Then the whole household will become much brighter."

Although the members of the plant all listened laughingly, there were many who soon tried out exactly what I said. Those people reported back to me in the following way:

"Up until now I would return home and yell, 'Isn't my food ready yet!' What I did was exactly opposite. I said gentle words and was as shy as if I was on stage in my first play, and it can be done. Thanks to you, our house has become very cheerful. The cooking has become delicious and the cleaning has made the house neat and tidy."

Then I would suggest, "Thank her by saying, 'My, the house has become so pretty.' Please practice putting your heart into your words."

Labor and Capital Depend on Human Esteem

The idea that if cash is invested interest will come back is not limited to married couples. When working as a plant manager I adapted the interest-on-love idea to company management.

To begin with, more important than anything is that the workers think as intimately of the plant as they do their homes. Also, as the plant manager, I think of the workers as members of my own family.

I employed one of the full-time plant carpenters to go to the house of each plant worker. I would have him fix the floors if they were rotten, put in new doors if they were broken or off the track, and repair everything in each household. Since the plant was one for processing wood, we could easily find extra wood for repairs. I said this to everyone:

"As you control your feelings and live pleasantly, brightly and congenially with your wives, please work hard. Let's all do much together. Work hard and raise the output of this plant. Then when that has happened I will hand out the plant dividends in thanks." At this plant, everyone worked seriously, the efficiency level went up and up, and we could have very good output. Even in the newspapers a big report was made of *The Plant of the Artist Manager.*

For a plant manager, maintaining warm person to person relations is very important. During our short lifetime, being devoted to the same task with everyone helping each other creates a deep refreshing feeling, and both the employee and the employer care about each other.

I think that present day labor and management confrontation is something belonging to the Stone Age of civilization.

About sixty people were employed in our plant. Everyone worked hard, but congenially. Since there was much excess lumber in the plant due to many unacceptable trees, everyone could have his house kept in repair by the company carpenter, and the feelings of the workers were positive and generous. I knew nothing of the technique of being a plant manager, but I thought of the workers as members of my own family. I thought of them as brothers. In the money of that time, I added 500 yen to the savings of each worker at the time of accounting. Five hundred yen was enough money to protect themselves for the time.

"If for some reason you need to spend more, please come to me. Then I will give you another 500 yen. Anyone who is able to increase their own savings, please do so. Such people are excellent." This is the kind of suggestion I made.

Since everyone felt secure in their life styles and had a great will to work, the efficiency level became even higher. I was a manager for only three years, but it was so much fun that even now it is a memory that I cannot forget.

Truth, Goodness, Beauty, and Love

Although I have talked about how wonderful the heart is in loving each other, respecting each other, and raising each other higher, it was while I was thinking deeply about this life that I became aware of the idea of *truth, goodness, beauty,* and *love.* While searching for life's *truth, goodness* and *beauty,* we will try to live in *love.*

If watched, even a dog understands beauty. It will never sleep on a muddy place. If there is a dry place, especially among grass, it will find the most desirable place to rest.

If let in the house, it will choose the neatest part of the sofa; if there are cushions, then it will curl up and sleep on top of the best one. The life workings of a dog unknowingly lead it to better and more desirable things. Again, when considering safety, if something unexpected comes, it will jump up at once and move. People are the same, and dogs are the same.

The life activity for survival seeks safer things and moves the self. Using *knowledge* to think of the end is not the same.

The same follows for the problem of goodness. Human life unconsciously seeks things more true and more beautiful. Even when looking at children play, this can be seen. Children naturally approach friends who are playing pleasantly.

No one thinks of the location of a murder as being pleasant. If one did, that person will have twisted himself away from the natural flow of life activity and have rationalized himself away from the normal flow of life.

Life desires to search for truer, better and more beautiful things. People try to live in abundant love while searching. What is life seeking? This is the question I always want to put at the foundation of my thinking.

When talking about the start and development of a talent, the most basic desire should be the search for truth, goodness, beauty and love. I suggested before that I want to compare exceptional talent with exceptional heart. This way of thinking of truth, goodness, beauty, and love is one big point in starting the development of talent.

What is life seeking?

You should put that in the center of your thoughts and raise your children correctly in life and talent.

Chapter 8

Develop Life

Use a Friendly Voice

Loving and having friends is what life strives for. Hating people is not what life is looking for. However, if hate is practiced daily, the talent for hating people grows.

If a person follows his own natural life activity, then he should always have a warm heart for people. Then if that is done, he should receive radiations from the warm hearts of others. In other words, the interest on love comes back.

In the juvenile prison, the following would often happen:

"Everyone, let's develop more ability to respect others and send love to others. With that in mind, first let's race to see who will be the first to say *Good Morning* each day. The one who says it first has more ability to send love to others. The one who says it first wins. A long time ago when a person greeted someone in Japanese with, 'It's early,' he answered with, 'I am late,' followed by, 'I am grateful for your generosity.' 'I am late,' means that I was late in greeting, so I lost. Well, starting tomorrow we are going to practice using friendly voices and being the faster in saying, *Good morning* or *Good night*. There are people who become offended if they are ignored after having said, *Good morning,* however this should not be. It is the other person who does not respond who is wrong. Because of that, you do not need to lose something by getting angry. If you consider that the other person is slightly deaf and could not hear you, or the other person does not have the ability to express love, then you will not be offended. But, to a person who ignores you, continue to say *Good morning* every day. The other person will surely come to look at you with a smile. That is the beginning of the returns on the *cash* you invested. Try to continue this greeting for ten days. Even the most eccentric person will eventually return a friendly voice with *Oh, good morning."*

To be able to express love is, of course, an ability, and to expand this ability it is necessary to practice continuously.

People who do not return a greeting after a person says, *Good morning* to them, are poor in this ability and are rather unfortunate fellows. People become angry saying, "You are conceited," when a greeting is not returned. But, do you become angry with a person for not being able to do mathematics well? When regarded as abilities, the expression of love and mathematics are both the same. Please invest more and more of the cash of love in a person who has no ability to express love. It may take a few days, but the interest will surely return. Using a friendly and loving voice is the easiest way.

Take a look at dogs. Even dogs who do not know each other approach each other and touch noses to smell each other. When they part, they will look back and wag their tails. Even as dogs greet each other and send love to each other, it would surely be good if humans could meet a stranger on the street and give a casual greeting.

If humans would recognize respect in each other and exchange expressions of love more, the world would be a brighter place.

The Ball of Friendship, the Ball of Hatred

A person makes his own lifestyle. It is not something that someone makes for him. A cheerful lifestyle is constructed by having a cheerful heart overflowing with love for other people. The lifestyle of a person who continues having love for others is a calm world with little trouble. The opposite of this is the lifestyle of the person who thinks good things about himself only and never thinks of doing services for other people. Such a lifestyle is a dark, turbulent one in which other people are unkind and seem to talk foolishness. Because no love-cash is invested, no interest comes back and trouble is invited.

The relationships between people are like the game of catch. If a person respects another and throws him a friendly ball, a friendly ball will be returned to him. If the person hates the other, a ball of hatred will be returned to him. This is the same as the words of Christ, "Do unto others as you would have them do unto you."

Do not wait to be shone upon (loved, respected, honored) by others, but be the first to invest love-cash. If the other person is a fine person, the investment and the interest will both be returned in full. If the other person does not have much ability for love, only the interest will be returned. If people would think in this way, they would never become offended.

When a wonderful friendship is returned, a person can feel that the other person has great ability for love. When even the interest is not returned, one knows the other person simply has no ability.

Feeling Happiness Is an Ability

It is exceedingly obvious that everyone is seeking happiness and that parents want happiness for their children.

What is happiness?

Happiness is not a thing. The very core of happiness is the human heart. Then there follows the ability to feel happiness in the heart. People who are seeking a thing are very happy when they receive that thing, but soon the heart changes and looks for the next better thing. There is no end. A person who has the ability to feel happiness can feel great happiness over small things.

For example, although I am breathing now it does not make me particularly happy. But, if someone went to the hospital and spent days by people who have asthma, he would feel thankful that he can breathe easily. At such a time a person can know happiness. It is possible to find much happiness even from little things. I think that parents unconsciously teach this happiness to their children.

For example, suppose five *ohagi** are received from the family next door. Although the parent said "Thank you," he says, while eating them, "Our neighbor is stingy and put in only a little sugar so it does not taste good," or complains, "They only gave us five. It would have been better if they had thought of the number of people in our family." This is teaching the ability of discontent to the children.

On the other hand, if the parent says, "The lady next door is so nice. She brought something she made herself to have us eat it. Let's eat because of her kindness," and ignores the bad taste, the children will eat it as if it were delicious. A child raised in this sort of atmosphere will be able to feel thankful. Even though it is the same *ohagi,* there is a great difference between the parent who teaches thankfulness and the parent who teaches discontent. Parents should know that even such small

*A type of rice cake.

things have a big influence on the development of a child. It is essential to take care, because there are parents who want happiness for their children yet raise them to be unable to feel happiness.

There are many people who always say unkind things like, "They should have watched more closely," behind the back of a person while saying "Thank you" to his face. Children absorb all of these actions and will do the same in their turn.

"Thank you" as lip service is very different from "Thank you" from the heart. The heart radiates differently. The other person can feel it if it is only lip service, and the flow of friendship between the two people is cut.

Unexpectedly, children absorb these things exactly. If a parent wants to teach a child to be thankful, the parent should show a thankful heart and allow the child to understand it naturally.

A Mother's Influence Is Great

The mother interacts with her child more than anyone. If the mother is an excellent person, the child will become an excellent person even though no special effort is made to do so. I think that the existence of woman is very noble. When bearing children, a woman has the duty of transmitting the human race into the next era. I think that womankind is a great asset to the human race. In the same way, the responsibility of birth is directly that of the mother.

Goethe said, "Eternity is seen in woman."

Nature has given woman the assignment of childbearing. Therefore, when raising children, the influence of the mother is greater than the influence of the father. Of course, the love and protection of the father goes together with the child-rearing of the mother.

It would be good if the father would reassure and encourage the mother every day. In a home where the father does so, parents and children can live happily together and the children will mature quickly. Even clocks need to be wound once a day. The father should give such reassurance to the mother every day with the same idea as winding a clock, even if he is shy. The pleasantness of each day will come out of this behavior. The continuation of the present is the future, and the present we have now will be the past at the next hour. We live in the present. Why not make it pleasant? Words of love are necessary for that purpose. Designing every day in happiness will result in a lifetime of happiness.

The Responsibility for Education Is in the Home

One day I went to an elementary school to observe. Just at that time there was a PTA meeting. The principal of the school greeted the mothers and asked for their continued cooperation in the home education of their children. Then the mothers thanked him and agreed to cooperate.

After listening to the exchange, I began to think that these people were a little crazy. The person who plants a seed in his field and cultivates it is the cultivator. Parents are cultivators. They are the ones responsible for raising their children with love. When the responsible person is asked to "cooperate" by the other person and agrees, it seems that the main and auxiliary roles are reversed. Something also seems wrong with the school teachers. If the neighbor of a farmer, who was caring for his own field, asked the farmer to "cooperate" in the care of that field, the farmer would become incensed. Nobody has the responsibility for bringing up a child to be a fine person except the parents of that child. It is the school teacher who should cooperate with the parents in educating the child. It is the parents who should be asking the teacher for cooperation and the school which should agree.

Remember that if a child commits a crime, it is the parents and not the teachers who are held responsible by the law. This one thing shows the responsibility of child education in the home.

Even so, there are parents who forget their duty to their children and indifferently leave the education of their children entirely up to the schools. Having ignored their children, the parents feel their responsibility for the first time when their children run up against the law. This is the retribution of cause and effect.

The First Duty Is Raising Your Child

The lives of American mothers are very busy with shopping and social functions. It is common for those mothers to think that when a child reaches a certain age his education can be left to the kindergarten.

In Japan, it is normal for the mother of a three-year-old violin student to come to the lessons, learn the violin, and teach the child at home. However, American mothers complain that they are very busy and do not have the time to take such care. Four or five years ago when I was in America, I heard the voices of mothers like that. Then my thoughts were bitter and I stood up from my seat at a workshop to talk to them.

"Of all the work that people do, there is nothing more noble, nothing more important, than raising your own child to be a fine person. Why do people have children if they are so busy they cannot take time to watch their children? If they are so busy, then why not wait until they have more free time to have children? You bear your own children. If so, then the duty of bringing them up well is imposed upon you. You say that you are very busy with social functions and shopping, but you must decide which is more important—such functions or bringing up your childen." I received vigorous applause from many teachers as they laughed. In the four or five years since then, the mothers of the American Talent Education have changed a great deal. Nowadays, everyone is very intense in the feeling that parents shape the fate of their children. I think that the mothers intelligently followed what I had said. I have been to America many times. Since I make that same speech every time I go, the mothers may have adopted a new way of thinking.

As a country, America is very earnest about the talent education of its children. The Talent Education project at Eastman School of Music in Rochester, New York, receives twenty thousand dollars every year from the state assembly as assistance money to manage the program. One hundred fifty children are a part of this educational experiment to research the opening up of new educatonal methods. There, the Suzuki method was taken and tried on the children. This is the third year.

It is very unfortunate that in Japan, few city councils take that budget and show the will to practice Talent Education. In New York, even my travel expenses when I go to lecture have been included in calculating the twenty thousand dollar grant from the state assembly.

When I went to Rochester the other day, a regional concert was held and 500 children performed on the violin in a gymnasium with a capacity for thousands of people. This concert took place on June 21, 1969. This is the expression of the success of the "Suzuki Method" in the violin talent education of small children. As in Japan, children of three and four years old developed quite well and showed good results. The happiness and emotions of the audience were tremendous. The movement to develop small children is being started in earnest in each state all over America.

Chapter 9

Look at Truth

Act When You Think

Often when we decide that something must be done, we put it off until the next day saying, "Well, starting tomorrow. . . ." People put things off until later saying that today is too busy and there is no time, when that is not true. Because of not doing things immediately, there are mountains of things left undone. In other words, in the end things do not get done.

Act when you think. This is what I call self discipline. I also often suggest it to other people.

I did something similar in my own home. Soon after the war when I had not been in Matsumoto long, my younger sister, her children, and Koji Toyoda lived with me. That winter was very cold with the temperature going down to minus 13 degrees Centigrade (about plus 7 degrees Fahrenheit). My sister returned from outside and said, "Brother, just now on the bridge in Honmachi, a soldier covered with cuts was standing in the snow. He was shivering as he asked for alms, but everybody was in such a hurry in the snow that nobody put any money in his box. I felt so sorry for him as I looked at him. I thought about wanting to put him under our nice warm *Kotatsu** table and serving him some delicious hot tea after standing in the snow on such a cold day."

---

*A low table with a heating element inside providing warmth to persons seated.

When I said, "You thought, didn't you?", my sister said, "Oh, that's right . . .," as she ran out the door. That was because at that time we had been practicing the words *Act when you think* in our household.

Twenty or thirty minutes later, my sister appeared in the front entry with the wounded soldier. Before that, Koji and the other children helped me warm up the room, and since we had just received some pastries from the Tokyo Nakamura shop, we got them out, prepared tea, and were waiting. When I greeted the man with, "Welcome," his eyes opened wide because this sort of thing had never before happened to him.

He greeted us saying, "I do not know what is going on, but as you said, 'Anyway, come and warm yourself at our house,' I will enter although I am imposing myself upon you." Then he entered the warm room and we all had a pleasant time eating pastries and drinking tea while sitting under the *Kotatsu* and telling folk tales.

The man said, "I had a wonderful time. When I go to Nagano I shall repay you."

Then I tried to put some extra money into his box, but he stayed my hand saying, "It would be wasteful to receive money from you when I have already received such care." Then jokingly I said, "It is because we made you rest that you lost the money you might have made," and I threw some money into his box and bade him leave.

Act when you think. Even now I cannot forget the memories of when our household practiced this idea. This was only one incident, but Koji and the other children always practiced the idea.

By acting when you think, things proceed very efficiently and the very air of the household comes alive. I also continue to tell myself about life and develop my life by thinking of life as one very important ability. If everyone did so in their own households, I guarantee that it would be easy and the home would become a pleasant and cheerful place.

Even if at first a person has to follow *Act when you think* consciously, the results of this training will give him the ability to do it and make it a habit. This ability has the power to change the life of a person.

The Speed of a Great Person Is Different

If I meet a person who does great work, I notice that the actions of such a person are different from those of normal people. Mr. Soichiro Ohara is one such person. I became very close to Mr. Ohara, who is a man with an agreeable disposition and a dream.

I had been hoping for something of this sort. I wanted someone very powerful in Japan who was also a fine person to think about the making of the Japan of tomorrow with early childhood development. I wanted to make a list of members like that in a kind of order.

Then I asked Mr. Ohara, "Would you choose a person from Japan. Choose a person who would think seriously about the Japan of tomorrow. Who do you think is best?"

Then Mr. Ohara said while thinking, "That's so, hmm," and already his hand was pushing a bell. His secretary came immediately.

Mr. Ohara said, "Get Mr. Ibuka," and two minutes later Mr. Ibuka was on the phone.

Mr. Ohara now said, "A Mr. Shinichi Suzuki is saying that he wants to visit you at around noon, so please meet him and speak with him about various things. I rely upon you," and hung up. Within five minutes, Mr. Ibuka called back and said, "Please come without eating so that we can talk over lunch." In this way everything is very efficient.

I soon met Mr. Ibuka and he was a wonderful person. Neither Mr. Ibuka nor Mr. Ohara ever gave an ambiguous answer like, "Let's set it aside to think about it a little while." If they cannot do something, they clearly say, "No," and if the answer is "Yes," then the speed of their actions is eye-opening. If they think that they can do something, they finish it off immediately right there.

If I meet Mr. Ibuka in Tokyo and ask him something saying, "Please help me with this," and he accepts it and says, "Yes, I understand," then, having returned to Matsumoto by train, I receive a notice from the person in charge saying, "The arrangements have been made, therefore. . . ." This is great speed.

People who are able to do great, large works do not say tedious things like, "Let us do it if there is time." If something is thought of, it is disposed of at once. That is a speed as quick as lightning. This is a very important thing in life.

We who do not have such an ability think, "I'll do it when I have free time," or "I'll do it tomorrow," because even while thinking that something must be done now, our attention moves to other things by habit. Even though we think of something, we are not moved immediately to action. The results are that it is always late.

Upon reflection, I told children that it was important to put into practice the thought "When you think of something, act," and I am trying to show by example how to do it.

I have noticed that if a person includes action when he thinks of something in every day life, and follows it for two or three years, then if the amount accomplished in one day or one month during that time is compared with the amount accomplished in one day or one month before that time, the amount accomplished during that time will be greater. There are many problems which would have been easily resolved, if they had been acted upon when they first came up. Such situations often are resolved too late because they are put off until the last minute, and then one has to rush to accomplish what is necessary. It is easy for us, who do not have the ability to act, to lose the chance for accomplishment.

Acting when a thought occurs is an ability. I think that we should develop it. If that can be done, life should be much fuller than at present. Life is practice. Life means continuing to train oneself and develop oneself by reflection.

We must think deeply about the fact that Casals, at ninety-one years old, even now practices the cello two hours every day so as not to be stagnant at even his high level of ability.

Even if someone becomes a fine person who does great works, he is not so exalted that he does not need to study. Rather the opposite is true, because he finds more and more problems to study and he has the will to grow higher and higher. He is in a world so advanced that we cannot even imitate him, but we learn that people train themselves more and reach for truer beauty.

A Handle for Reflection

Quickly reflecting that, *this must be done* is connected with *act quickly on what you think*. This reflection is also an ability. It is even possible to say that greater or lesser ability for reflection is an important point for creating superior or inferior human abilities.

At seventeen or eighteen, the physical development of the brain stops and a person enters the adult world. In the adult world, a person holds the handle for self-reflection, repairs himself, and must walk while developing himself more.

If a parent did not give the child this handle on reflection, the child would not be able to continue to develop himself, and his life would end as a dull one. The ability to reflect needs to be internalized by children through their upbringing. Parents should begin by being a good example.

For instance, it is important in everyday life for parents to say things like, "Oh, I was wrong. From now on I will not do that again."

A person who cannot harmonize well with other people is one who cannot see that he is ever wrong or convey a contrite attitude. Such a person always says that the other person is wrong, society is wrong, and he always rebukes anything but himself. He has not once said that he himself was wrong.

Growth begins when a person becomes able to reflect upon his wrong doings. Human growth is completed upon a reflective base. This is a very important ability.

Reaching for truth occurs when a heart looks at the mistakes made previously, and opens up new ways of looking at truth. Then one can say that the talent of reflection was as high as that of an educated person. Also, the power to reach truth will grow to be as much as that of a great person.

Reflection is not something that should be pushed on another by saying, "Reflect!" It is something a person uses himself. It is thinking deeply about oneself. It is convenient to use it saying, "You must reflect!", but if used in that way the results are likely to display the talent of contradiction in the other person who will say, "Reflection? Who needs it!"

In the process of bringing up their children, parents should take care that the children develop the talent for reflection. If the parents think that their children do not have that talent, then the parents should demonstrate how they reflect that they were wrong, and thus naturally instruct their children.

In the story I told of a mother holding her obstinate child and crying with him in the storage house, the mother had a very high reflective talent. That feeling will surely be transferred to the child. The child of such a mother will mature quickly.

The Base of a Triangle

A baby grows while absorbing all of his environment. If that growth were shown by a drawing, it would be a triangle. The period from infanthood to toddlers, the period in which everything in the environment is absorbed, is the base of the triangle. As the child grows bigger, his power to absorb the environment becomes less, and the triangle becomes narrower toward the top until it is completed.

By making himself better through reflection and judgment, the adult makes up for having little power to absorb from his surroundings. Therefore, the human form regarding reflection and judgment starts small and grows, like an inverted triangle.

The power of the young to catch their surroundings is truly wonderful. They develop human characteristics before you know it in the blink of an eye. Yesterday cannot be repeated. Because that method of forming is so fast, regrettably there are many times we cannot keep up with it. Humans taking on human form are similar to a plaster sculpture. At first, it is wet and gooey. The plaster soon hardens. After the hardened form is made, nothing can be changed about it. The heart and talents of a person are the same.

Let me tell about one interesting side of the process and the speed of making talent. A four or five year old kindergartener is taught a *Haiku** (at the Talent Education kindergarten in Matsumoto). Even the slowest child will memorize the poem after forty repetitions. After two months, the child has the ability to memorize one poem and eventually easily memorizes two poems per day. Then, after one year, the child is very easily able to say one hundred seventy to two hundred poems one after the

*A seventeen syllable Japanese poem.

other. This ability is an awesome thing. In children, the talent to remember something after hearing it only once is cultivated.

The same can be said for violin practice. After the first piece is internalized, train some more and add the next piece. Master it and add the next. *Keep every piece learned* [emphasis added] so that it can be played at any time. This is not just the power of memorization, but the power of internalization. If this method of development is used, the child will remember things well. For instance, a child will memorize a telephone number as something interesting. Because I soon forget, I tell a child, "Remember this telephone number for me." Three or four days later when I think I must telephone the person, I call the child who was to remember the telephone number and he remembers it with no trouble. I cannot keep up with such memories.

These children are receiving much memory training. It is one talent cultivated when they are very little. They do not try to memorize, but something sticks to them and stays there as a strong memory. I think that one can soon see the difference between people who internalized the ability to memorize when they were at the base of the triangle at a very young age, and people who did not.

All Movements Memorized

This is the story of Koji Toyoda when he was fourteen years old. At that time, Koji was living with me in Matsumoto and Kenji Kobayashi had come to visit us for a week. Both of them were fine boys and good friends.

At that time, there was a request from the Matsumoto NHK radio station, "We would like the two of them to perform on the violin." I secretly thought in my heart that I would test the two of them.

There is a piece by Vivaldi entitled *Concerto for Two Violins in A minor*. This is a very difficult piece

which is divided into three movements. The performance
time totals about twenty minutes. I thought I would test
their ability by having them play that piece. Then I
answered the radio station saying, "They will play *Concerto for Two Violins*," and did not tell the boys anything.

On the morning of the day before the broadcast, I
called the boys together and for the first time I told them,
"There was an offer from NHK. Tomorrow afternoon at
one o'clock you are playing the Vivaldi *Concerto for Two
Violins* at NHK." I showed them the music saying,
"Study this today," and gave it to them at which time
they said, "Oh no, this is terrible!", and they ran into
their room holding their heads.

Maybe an hour and a half had passed. Thinking
that I would like to check them on some problems of
expression, I entered the room in which they were practicing. And, what had happened?

They had memorized the first movement and were
playing it beautifully. I admired them for such a wonderful thing. At that time I left the room after checking only
very simple things and by evening they had memorized all
of the movements and were performing without looking
at the music.

At noon the next day, a car came from the broadcasting station to pick them up. "Today, I will listen to
you on the radio, so you two go ahead. But before you go,
play it once," I said, and the two of them put the music
on my desk, stood on the other side of the room and began
to play. Without using the music, all movements were
played very fluently.

"It's just fine now. Go and play your best."

"Yes sir, here we go," they said, and left.

The music was left on my desk. Neither of them had
any thought of taking the music with them. When I
listened to them on the radio, it was a truly wonderful
performance. Although I was very surprised, I really was
sure that they could do it.

(We cannot keep up with such things. If we were in the same situation, we would have to practice very earnestly for about one month, and even so, at performance time we would be very nervous and keep the music nearby to look at. Those children arrived at such heights because they had been brought up with the habit of memorizing the music they saw and playing without looking at it from the time they were very little.)

When a habit of memorization is really internalized, something that is uncommon for us can be done as if it were very common. It is nothing to them. To the two of them, that talent has always existed.

This is one incident which again makes me feel that a talent internalized when a child is very small is a talent which can easily manifest itself even when others are watching.

(For the record, Koji Toyoda is now the concertmaster of the Berlin Symphony Radio Orchestra, and Kenji Kobayashi is the concertmaster of the Oklahoma Symphony Orchestra in America.)*

Speak With the Grandparents

If the parents recognize how important human development is from birth and raise their children with love, the children will grow up as happy human beings because it has been accomplished by the parents.

Of those parents, the mother has the strongest hold upon her child's fate. However, sometimes the grandparents will live together in the same household. If they are wonderful grandparents, then of course this is a big plus to the human development of the child.

However, sometimes no matter how firmly decided the mother is about raising her child, the grandparents,

*As of 1968

through what we might call blind love, think the child is very cute, and they dote upon him. In such cases, the child takes being loved for granted and insists upon being loved more and more. The feeling that he is not being loved enough is started in his heart.

At such times, the parents and the grandparents must confer. Often mothers say to me, "Grandmother is such a problem. But it is difficult to tell her so because she is my mother-in-law." However, this situation will be a lifetime problem for the child.

We must talk with grandmothers and grandfathers in order to make a good home environment. Let's follow the saying, "Act when you think." Worrying about the problem will not help. As you worry, the child will continue to absorb from the environment.

First one must have a family meeting. Then the child's mother could say the following:

"For some reason, our child desires attention for himself and does not know how to do things for others. I would like to do many more things for all of you, and I would like my child to be aware of this kindness towards others. I would appreciate your help."

If said in this way, Grandmother surely will not say, "My son's wife is impertinent."

Grandparents do not have the right to complain about and scold their daughter-in-law. But, they have the privilege to request things for and confer about their grandchild.

If the mother says, "I would like to try doing this. Would you help me?", then the grandparents should understand because they also want the child to be happy. Being frank and saying in conference, "For our child, let's make this home the best environment," is something that can be done in any household.

Then as the child watches his mother being kind to his grandparents, the feeling of consoling elderly people will be born naturally. Soon, being courteous to his parents, minding his manners, and being kind to other people will be taken for granted in the child's heart.

Even Siblings

I am often asked why children born of the same parents have different personalities.

Many people insist that people being raised in the same environment, but having different personalities, shows that talent is inborn after all. However, there is a basic error made when one assumes that the same environment is involved.

When the first baby is born, only his mother and father are at his side. Suppose the next child is born when the first child has reached the age of three. The younger child is raised surrounded by his mother, his father, and his older brother or sister.

Looking only at this fact, the environment of the first child is greatly different from that of the second. The first child is carefully watched by his parents who tend to be overly protective. Therefore, it is easy for the first child to be unenergetic, quiet, and the *proverbial dunce.**

For the second child, however, a three year old sister or brother is around even when he is asleep. Sometimes his face will be pushed. Sometimes his nose will be pinched. Because he must defend himself, he will be strong-willed. In order to defend himself, his power to train himself will be quite strong. Just like the proverb, "The soul of a three-year-old child lasts until he is one-hundred." If the small child trains to defend himself everyday, he will have a very strong character.

The environment of the third child is even more complicated. There are two older children nearby, and the relationship of the mother and father is not as pure

*"The first child is a dunce" is a Japanese proverb.

as when they were newlyweds, but now includes some shadows.

Therefore, even for brothers and sisters, one can never say that each has had the same environment. On a large scale one can say that no two people in the world are raised in the same environment.

I can even talk about this from the viewpoint of playing the violin. The older child starts violin lessons and continues playing the violin a great deal. At this point the younger child is born. The baby is nurtured while listening to his elder brother or sister practicing. Therefore, the baby memorizes more and more pieces. Soon, when the baby becomes a three-year-old, he starts the violin and moves considerably faster than the older child.

Then the parent says, "For some reason the younger child seems to be smarter." This is a *common mistake* which has existed for a long time. Because violin music was in the environment from an early age, of course the child will learn quickly.

The same can be said about words. In a household containing only a child and his parents, of the father goes to work and the mother is a quiet person who does not spend much time visiting with neighbors, the child will have little chance to hear words. Naturally, the child will begin to speak at a later age.

However, for the second child, there is a mother who speaks to him and near him as well as an older brother or sister of three or four years old. Therefore, the second child will begin to say "Mama" at an earlier age. Because this child is more precocious, his parents are quick to say, "This child is much better than the older one."

The third child will learn even faster than the second, notice details, and will seem quite wise.

Although the method in which the first child receives stimulation is quite different, it is only normal.

Sometimes I hear a person say, "If you look at all three of our children, the third is the smartest," but it also can be shown that there is a definite reason. They were brought up that way. I would like parents to accept this reasoning and avoid grading their children as *A, B, C,* or *D.*

One should not become the kind of unreasonable parent who decides to make one child study hard because he is the most likely to become a success. It is necessary to think carefully in order to ascertain true potentials of a child.

Know Humans

In addition to raising children, the most important thing on which to spend one's time is *knowing human beings.*

Maybe it is better to say *understanding or ascertaining human beings.*

I will take an example from a child's violin study for thought. A child who listens to the record every day at home and is raised following my directions has a polished musical sense and moves very quickly when he starts the violin. However, a child who has not listened to the record, and who is forced to practice after his mother complains, will not polish his music sense and makes very little, if any, progress.

"My child does not seem to be good at music," says his mother, and has him learn to draw. Then, the child quickly draws any old thing which happens to be a good picture.

"See, my child is good at drawing," says his mother. However, that is to be expected because the mother does not stand over the child and complain when he draws. He can freely have a relaxed and pleasant time in the world of drawing.

With the violin, hearing his mother say, "Hey, posture!", "Hey, hand position," is very pesky. Because in drawing, the child can escape from such a troublesome environment, the picture can be drawn boldly. The parent misunderstands this and says that the child is better at drawing.

This story, and others like it, is a good example of how little parents know their children or are able to understand human beings.

One cannot look at a small child and randomly choose what he does well and what he does poorly. I have repeated many times that more important than whether one *is talented* or not is a good environment in which a child will *become talented*.

The Seashore Test Is Outdated

There was a famous psychologist named Seashore. Mr. Seashore devised a test of musical aptitude called he Seashore Test. This test can be given to four and five year olds to see if they are musically inclined or not.

A long time ago this test had authority and was accepted as proof that musical talent was inborn.

A few years ago when I went to America, I was asked, "Mr. Suzuki, what do you think of the Seashore Test?" I answered in this way:

"Don't ask my opinion about that, you should ask Mr. Seashore. How do you test children in America for an inclination to speak English?"

My answer must have sounded sarcastic for everyone laughed very hard. What I wanted to say was the following:

Any child has the possibility to be musically inclined. Talent will sprout according to how the children are raised. Testing a child for musical inclination is illogical. It is the same as testing a child born in America for the inclination to speak English. In my opinion, the Seashore Test is the psychology of the last century.

The research of some scholars seems very scientific while having holes in it.

For example, scholars often say the following about identical twins:

"What would happen if identical twins were raised in exactly the same environment? This is important research." However, there is one mistake in those words. A person who has kept my opinions in his heart should know. There is no such thing as two environments exactly the same.

For example, even if identical twins are clothed identically, and given the same meals at the same table every day, there will be something different about them.

If one child drops his bowl and it breaks, his mother will say, "That's no good. Be more careful." If she does not then scold the other child, one cannot say that the children are in precisely the same environment.

Even if the other child is scolded, that child had not broken his bowl so his feelings will become mixed when he is scolded. In which case, no matter what one says, they were not raised in exactly the same environment.

One can understand that even the slightest thing will make a psychological difference in their development. Even if a mother says, "I nurtured them in exactly the same way . . .," that is not true.

On top of raising children, I would like you to think about how important the key *Knowing the truth* is from this example.

I have spent many words communicating what I understand from my experience about the talent development of children.

The talent of a child is not inborn. Any child has the sprout of possibility to grow. If a child is left alone, his talent will wither. Please! For noble children, ascertain the truth, nurture that sprout with overflowing love, and make the flower of hope bloom.

Any child, every child will surely grow wonderfully.

It depends upon how they are raised. "The fate of a child is in the hands of his parents."

Please, prepare the best environment for your child. Parent and child should grow together looking towards the future. I pray for your happiness.

If this book becomes a light of hope for mothers who love their children and wish for them to grow up wonderfully, I could not be happier.

THE END